A Spectacle of the Highest Celebrity..

. . This is the engaging phrase coined by two artists who were among the first of many from outside India who have recorded the Taj Mahal in words, on canvas and paper, and in photographs. The artists, Thomas Daniell and his nephew William, arrived in Agra in 1789 and sketched furiously for a few days. Later, back in London, they published their work with a little booklet in which this phrase appears. There is more about the two artists in the pages which follow.

'A spectacle of the highest celebrity' is a lovely description which in more leisurely days would have made an apt title for a book such as this. Today we must get straight to the point. So, In Praise of the Taj Mahal. Not praise in the sense of just one extravagant comment after another but in the form of an honest description which may help lead to understanding.

The Taj Mahal is a difficult building to comprehend. It is the only substantial monument to a woman who was not also a ruler anywhere in the world. It was erected to honour a woman we scarcely know, in part of the world where women were and are still subservient. It was built by an emperor many still regard as an alien intruder.

Yet the Taj Mahal has become both a symbol of India and a symbol of romance. It leaves its mark, one way or another, on more than a million visitors each year. It is a building truly with a tale to tell.

In Praise of the Taj Mahal

by
Hugh Mabbett

Photographs by
Fiona Nichols

JANUARY BOOKS

Published by January Books Ltd
35 Myrtle Crescent,
Wellington, New Zealand.

© January Books Ltd 1989

ISBN 0-9597806-5-3

Correspondence should be sent to
Design Business (S) Pte Ltd
809 French Road, #06-160
Singapore 0820.

Designed by
Design Business (Singapore) Pte Ltd

Colour-Separation by
Magenta Lithographic Consultants
Singapore

Printed by
Art Printing Works Sdn Bhd
Kuala Lumpur, Malaysia

What did the great lovers look like? There is no problem with Shah Jahan, whose whole life was recorded in detail. The painting on the left, reproduced by courtesy of the Board of Trustees of the Victoria and Albert Museum in London, shows him at the age of twentyfive (about 1616) when he was still known as Prince Khurram. He must have been pleased with it, because the inscription across the bottom, in his own hand, says: 'A good portrait of me . . . and a fine work by Nadir-uz-Zaman.'

It was painted at Ajmer, where his father Jahangir held court for three years, and is described in Dr Asok Kumar Das' book, *Splendour of Mughal Painting*, as follows: Against a dark background, the young, ambitious and highly successful prince stands with a poised and aristocratic air in a flowering meadow, wearing rich jewellery and holding an aigrette of European design.' An aigrette is a piece of jewellery in imitation of a plume of feathers.

At that time Prince Khurram, who would shortly earn his title Shah Jahan in battle, had been married about four years to Mumtaz Mahal, who gained her title at the time of their wedding. She had already borne him four children, one of whom, their first, died at the age of three.

But while we know so much about the husband, we know little about the wife — not even what she looked like. Dr Asok Kumar Das and other authorities say they do not know of a single authentic painting of her. Women artists (male artists were not allowed into the harem) may have made portraits of her, but none is known to exist.

Who then is the comely person in the picture above, who is routinely called Mumtaz Mahal? Versions of this portrait are widely used in books and on souvenirs, but we have no way of judging its accuracy. Possibly it derives from copies of an authentic portrait which has been lost. Or the first painting in this form may have been created by an artist with no knowledge at all of what Mumtaz looked like. The version reproduced here is by Akhtar Hussein, of Delhi, who follows a family tradition of painting on ivory, and is published by permission of Kohinoor Jewellers, Agra.

Many people helped produce this book. Special thanks are due to Mr R.M. Puri, director of the Government of India Tourist Office in Singapore, to his colleagues in Delhi, and to Mr R.C. Khandelwal and his staff in the department's Agra office. We were fortunate also to receive much assistance from Air India, on the ground and in the air, and from senior officers of the Archaeological Survey of India offices in Delhi and Agra, especially Mr M.C. Joshi, the ASI's joint director general. Others who were unstinting with information and assistance in other ways include Mr Rajesh Lal and Mr V.K. Suri of Lauries Hotel in Agra, Mr Kuldeep Narain, Mrs Ravi Sandhu, Mr M.A. Khan, Mr S.N. Singh, Mr Ghanshyam Mathur, Mrs Shantona Poduval, Mr Ashok Kumar Jain, the staffs of the libraries of the Times of India and India Today, and Mr Michael Sweet, of Antiques of the Orient in Singapore, for assistance in finding old prints and descriptions. Tribute must also be paid to Mr Muni Lal, journalist, diplomat, cricketer and biographer, whose book on Shah Jahan (New Delhi, 1986) has been invaluable. More helpful people and organisations are mentioned in the pages which follow.

Lauries Hotel, our base in Agra for several weeks, deserves mention in its own right. It is one of the oldest hotels in Asia, built in 1854 to cater not only to official and commercial travellers but also to tourists even in those days drawn to the Taj Mahal. Though no longer luxurious, Lauries' original character has been well preserved, and it also now has a swimming pool (supplied from the hotel's own well) which helped us through the heat of early summer. There have long been plans to restore Lauries to its original eminence in Agra, despite competition from a rash of new hotels which enjoy the economies of modern design. It is to be hoped the growing tide of tourists will enable it to put these plans into effect. Even as it is, however, we found Lauries a pleasant place to come home to.

Contents

How not to see the Taj Mahal

The tourists gathered before dawn in the shouting turmoil of the New Delhi railway station on that chilly winter morning were easy to pick out from the Indian commuters. They had brighter clothes, swinging shoulder bags instead of briefcases, and cameras; and they formed a nub of excitement where the 'air-conditioned chair class' carriages were expected to stop when their train pulled in. They were restless as all good travellers are as they embark on something new.

On this January morning they were embarking on the Taj Express, which leaves Delhi at 7am each day for Agra, city of the Taj Mahal, and Gwalior, city of a famous mediaeval fortress. The trip south-southeast to Agra takes about three hours, giving tourists about nine hours there to see the Taj and other sights before boarding the train for the trip back to Delhi in the evening.

Such is the reputation of the Taj Express outside India that I had assumed it was designed primarily for tourists, with fittings to match. Finding our names on a computer printout posted at the door to our carriage tended to confirm that we were getting special treatment, until I learned that Indian railway reservation systems are increasingly computerised. Then I realised that the great majority of pas-

The Taj Mahal, perpetually changing with the hours and the seasons, is a building to reflect on. Actual reflections make it still more alluring.

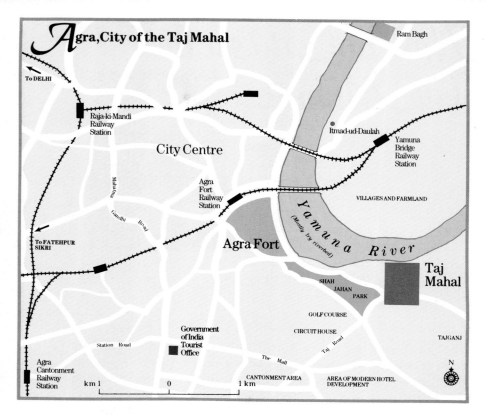

Agra, City of the Taj Mahal

Ram Bagh

To DELHI

Raja-ki-Mandi
Railway
Station

Itmad-ud-Daulah

Yamuna
Bridge
Railway
Station

City Centre

Agra
Fort
Railway
Station

VILLAGES AND FARMLAND

To FATEHPUR
SIKRI

Agra Fort

Yamuna River
(Mostly dry riverbed)

Taj
Mahal

SHAH
JAHAN
PARK

GOLF COURSE

CIRCUIT HOUSE

Government
of India
Tourist
Office

Station Road

The Mall

Taj Road

TAJGANJ

N

Agra
Cantonment
Railway
Station

km 1   0   1 km

CANTONMENT AREA

AREA OF MODERN HOTEL
DEVELOPMENT

sengers were Indian, and that the train was not noticeably different
from the hundreds of others which range India. On all of them you
drink similar tea, are served similar rice and chapatti meals and meet
a diversity of Indian travellers. The Taj Express is not a tourist special at all.

In fact, compared with trains which cover great distances to link
the huge cities of the sub-continent — Delhi, Bombay, Calcutta,
Madras — the Taj Express is little more than a suburban conven-
ience. In the weeks which followed my first train journey to Agra I
found that others throughout the day are just as fast and convenient,
offering virtually the same facilities. Getting to the city of the Taj
Mahal is no problem, even if you lack imagination enough to fly to
Agra or travel by bus or taxi.

The train pulls out, smooth as silk. Its route to Agra lies first
through the industrial slums which surround Delhi and then through
countryside, garden-like with crops, busy with harvesting or blasted
by the summer sun depending on the season. Through tinted glass
you see 'the real India' of low-lying villages and buffalo beside

waterholes and women in colourful saris walking down lanes, water jar on head. Wherever you look there are people.

Agra's main station is called Agra Cantonment, a name redolent of the past because 'cantonment' means an area assigned specially to military use; the English started it and the Indians carry it on. The Cantonment area is still distinct from the rest of the city, with its own local government and tidier streets. A sign in the station advises tourists to alight for the Taj Mahal and other monuments.

And so those travellers who left Delhi before dawn embark upon the real point of their visit to Agra, in many cases the point of their visit to this country. The Taj is India. It identifies the country. It is probably the most famous building in the world. It is the outstanding tourist attraction, featured in virtually all publicity material, known by reputation in advance by virtually all visitors. Were it a commercial logo, it would be the most successful of all time. Many visitors design their entire Indian tours around an excursion to see the Taj. India without the Taj is unthinkable.

However, most of those who plan to catch the Taj Express back to Delhi in the evening will spend more time visiting those 'other monuments' of that railway station sign than they will at the Taj Mahal. They will be taken to Fatehpur Sikri, an astonishing deserted ruin out in the countryside; and to Agra Fort, a huge and fascinating place; and perhaps to Itmad-ud-Daula, an enchanting mausoleum. There will be lunch somewhere as well, and the day will slip by so fast that time at the Taj, when the visitors eventually get there, will be as little as half an hour. No guide, no matter how expert, can do justice to this building in such a short time; and no visitor, no matter how intent on seeing as much as possible as quickly as he can, can really appreciate it. The Taj needs time.

Thus it is, as the Taj Express rolls back north to Delhi through the darkening countryside, that some visitors are a little thoughtful. They had seen the Taj Mahal, which had much to do with their being in India at all — but had they seen enough of it? 'I was asked to take a visiting prime minister's wife to the Taj, and was told to get her in and out in twenty-five minutes,' a guide told me. 'I said it was impossible. I kept her

there for fortyfive minutes — and then she stayed for another half hour before she could be dragged away.'

However, not all of us are prime minister's wives who can defy our programmes even by less than an hour. Most of us let ourselves be chivied about like sheep. Seeing the Taj Mahal like sheep is not the way. With all respect to the excellent Taj Express or to the new and faster trains which began running late in 1988, a day trip to Agra and all its offerings is not enough.

The best way to arrive at the Taj Mahal is with time to spare, and by three-wheeled cycle rickshaw. Having time to spare will slow you down, and so will riding in one of Agra's thousands of rickshaws, which comfortably take two passengers. You proceed down the Mall at a stately rate, sitting so high that you have a vantage point on Cantonment life. The man powering your machine will almost certainly try to engage you in conversation, to pass the time, to induce a tip, or to persuade you to visit one of Agra's hundreds of shops catering to tourists with carpets, marble inlay work, leather goods, jewellery or other trivia. If he succeeds in delivering you to a shopkeeper's door, he will get a small commission; if you buy something, a much larger one. Some rickshawmen will take you aboard for nothing if you agree to go shopping. Today you are not shopping. You are going to the Taj Mahal.

But you do not go all the way by rickshaw. You get off at the entrance to Shah Jahan Park (formerly Victoria Park at one end, MacDonnell Park at the other). There are pleasant walks amid the trees, at the right times of the year there are flowers galore, and you may see peacocks on the grass, vultures amid the branches and other birds everywhere. You will certainly see the Taj Mahal looming white and shapely above its surrounding walls. It is a first impression which will enhance rather than diminish your later, closer familiarity with this astonishing building.

You walk down the hill, past the waiting rickshaws and their motorised brethren — since you are arriving their drivers will leave you alone — and along the short road to the west gate. Since you have your mind and eyes on as much of the Taj as you can still see above its tall surrounding walls, you more easily ignore the hawkers trying to sell you drinks, postcards, film, jewellery, handcrafts, snacks. Unless it is a Friday, when admission is free, you buy entry tickets for two rupees, a few cents, per person at a little window to the left of the gate. It must be one of the world's best buys.

A quarter of your two rupees goes to the Archaeological Survey of India, the government department which owns and maintains the Taj Mahal, and the rest to the Agra Development Authority, which is charged with beautifying a city badly in need of it. When we were working on this book, no solution had been found to the apparently

---

Much literature about the Taj Mahal deals not with the building itself but with what people have made of it. Most of this writing involves praise, and long passages of praise, no matter how cleverly done, can be boring reading. This book's selection of great purple passages from the past, therefore, is spread lightly through the pages which follow. They are in no particular order, and there is a little criticism as well.

The series begins with perhaps the most extravagant comment of them all. It is by Mrs Sleeman, the wife of a British officer, later Major-General Sir William Sleeman, who organised the suppression of India's Thugs, dedicated murderers calculated to be slaying 30,000 travellers a year. He is a noted figure in Indian history — but his wife's remark has made her rather more famous than he:

I cannot tell you what I think [she said], for I know not how to criticise such a building, but I can tell you what I feel. I would die tomorrow to have such another over me.

---

simple problem of combining these fees into a single ticket. The task of combining their collection seemed equally intractable. We got two tickets each and handed them over separately to two men to be torn in half. An average of about five thousand people a day go through this process, or about one and half million a year, though free entry on Fridays and for children makes figures difficult to pin down. Record attendance on any one day is more than twenty thousand.

There is no way of knowing how many visitors to the Taj Mahal are foreign tourists, but it is a fair bet that a high proportion of visitors to India get there eventually. In 1987 India received more than a million of them. More than one hundred and sixty thousand came from Britain, more than one hundred and thirty thousand came from the United States. West Germany and France sent more than sixty thousand each, Japan and Italy more than forty thousand, and Canada, Australia and the United Arab Emirates more than thirty thousand each. The total goes up each year.

Between buying your tickets for the Taj Mahal and getting to the ticket collecting stage, you pass through a huge gateway into the fore-court, a spacious area with some shops, lawns, trees, wide paved areas and, well, space. There are people coming and going, and touts promoting their nearby shops. You get your first impression of the vast appeal that the Taj Mahal exercises on Indians as well as on other people. Visitors come from all over this vast country, so you see not only fashionable holiday makers but villagers from remote places, dressed much as they would be at home, many barefooted and bangled, the women colourful with handmade saris, heavy with

cheap jewellery, the men striding handsomely behind their inevitable moustaches. There will be people from the mountains and the plains, and perhaps Muslim women so heavily veiled that you wonder if they can see the Taj Mahal at all. The great majority of Indian visitors travel in family groups, often three or four generations in one party. Even the forecourt can be totally engaging.

You come to an even larger gateway, a monumental building in its own right. Late last century E.B. Havell, author of a tourist handbook to Agra and its surroundings, commented: 'It is well to pause before

The great gateway to the Taj Mahal is often disregarded in favour of the Taj. From either side, as on these two pages, it warrants attention.

Perfect symmetry enhanced by water. Cleverly placed reflecting pools give the Taj an extra dimension.

Did you ever build a Castle in the Air? Here is one, brought down to earth, and fixed for the wonder of ages; yet so light it seems, so airy, and, when seen from a distance, so like a fabric of mist and sunbeams, with its great dome soaring up, a silvery bubble, about to burst in the sun, that, even after you touched it, and climbed to its summit, you almost doubt its reality. — Bayard Taylor, an American novelist and journalist, in A Visit to India, China and Japan, 1855.

The whole appears like a most perfect pearl on an azure ground. The effect is such, I confess, I never experienced from any work of art. The fine materials, the beautiful forms, and the symmetry of the whole, with the judicious choice of situation, far surpasses anything I ever beheld. — William Hodges, English painter, who visited Agra in 1782.

entering and admire the proportions and perfect taste of the decoration of this gateway; for afterwards one has no eye for anything but the Taj itself.' It is more than thirty metres high, a towering central arch with lofty wings on each side, a row of marble cupolas on top and much inlaid Islamic text and floral decoration. It is worth a second glance.

You enter the cool and shadowy space beneath that towering arch. One of your two tickets is torn in half, your bag is searched as if you were about to board a plane, and your second ticket is torn in half. There is talk of installing an airport-type metal detector to meet terrorist threats to blow up the Taj Mahal, but during our weeks in Agra it seemed to draw no nearer.

While all this is going on, the Taj is waiting, gleaming at the other end of the tunnel-like main entrance, shimmering white against the sky 'like a greeting from another world'. There is a trick here. If the crowd is sparse enough, if security people accept your indication that you are going out only to return, stand outside the gateway on a line which leads directly to the Taj itself. Only a small part of it will be visible. Then walk slowly forward, keeping to that central line through the tunnel, so that gradually the Taj is revealed to you in its total majesty. That is an experience; and you may also find that as you move from shadow into light the building appears to float; and that is another experience.

Time and again visitors to the Taj Mahal have commented on its lightness, on the manner in which it is huge and solid yet also ethereal and weightless. We met an Indian family from the English Midlands who were showing their ten-year-old son something of the country they had left. Asked about the Taj, the boy commented that 'it seemed to have no foundations'; meaning that it was not pinned to the earth as all other buildings are but that it floats in a dimension of its own.

Passing through the inner archway is like bursting into space. There stands the Taj Mahal against the sky, there spread the gardens all around, the white and blue and green decorated by plots of flowers in pastel colours and by the garments of the visitors strolling here and there. It is a picture to dwell upon. 'When I bring tourists here I try to tell them the history of the Taj Mahal,' a guide told us, 'but they tell me to keep quiet. They just want to look.' There are reports of people crying, or being so moved that they must sit down.

History comes later (if not earlier) but it must come. There is no real appreciation of the Taj Mahal without some knowledge also of its story. Whether it is the true story or the embroidered version that

For a century and a half after it was built, the Taj Mahal remained unknown in Europe except through unreliable travellers' tales. This changed around

the end of the Eighteenth Century. An English artist named William Hodges reached Agra around 1782, and painted the first picture of the Taj which we know of. It is reproduced here by permission of the National Gallery of Modern Art in New Delhi.

Hodges recorded his impression that the Taj 'appears like a most perfect pearl on an azure ground'. The effect, he added, 'is such, I confess, I never experienced from any work of art. The fine materials, the beautiful forms, and the symmetry of the whole, with the judicious choice of position, far surpass anything

DRAWN & ENGRAVED BY THOS & W.M DANIELL.

THE TAJE MAHEL, AGH

I ever beheld.' He found the foun-
tains playing and the gardens 'in
tolerable repair'.

Hard on his heels came two
more Englishmen, Thomas
Daniell and his young nephew

William, who reached Agra in 1789. Their two paintings here are reproduced by courtesy of the Trustees of the British Museum. The two men pitched their tents on the north bank of the Yamuna

river, opposite the Taj Mahal, and settled down to sketching the monument. The next day they crossed the river and began work inside the Taj grounds. Thomas Daniell used a camera obscura, a forerunner of photography in which light passing through a tiny hole projects images on to paper for the artist to trace. Two days later the Daniells moved on to drawing the Fort, Akbar's tomb and Fatehpur Sikri. They had good reason for working so fast — the countryside was unsettled and their camp was attacked twice.

Back in England in 1794, they settled down to turning their hundreds of drawings into aquatints and publishing them over the next five years. Later, in 1801, they published the two prints shown here, with a booklet which included a ground plan of the monument and its surroundings, which is shown on pages 34 and 35.

In their booklet the Daniells observed that the Taj Mahal, 'a spectacle of the highest celebrity,' was visited by people of all ranks and from all parts. 'This high admiration,' they continued, 'is however not confined to the partial eye of the Indian native; it is beheld with no less wonder and delight by those who have seen the productions of art in various parts of the globe. . . . We were overwhelmed with its effect.'

So attractive were the Daniells' aquatints, and so exotic was their subject, that they remained popular for decades — and then were so much in demand that they became rare and expensive.

some guides favour does not much matter, so long as it is understood that an epic is represented here, not just of love as the more romantic accounts would have it but also of adventure, drama and power. Were it fiction it would belong not on this earth but in outer space, on some far planet much given to strangeness. The story of the Taj Mahal is just as unworldly as its appearance.

This the visitor may begin to appreciate as he (which for the purposes of this book includes she) walks slowly down the central aisle, along the lines of cypress trees standing like gloomy mourners, through the gardens to the main building. Inside there are two tombs. In one is buried a woman who in many details is almost unknown, a name without even a face to go with it, or a personality, but whose name, Mumtaz Mahal, will live for ever in the slightly corrupted form of Taj Mahal. In the other, alongside, lies her husband, a man who ruled a mighty empire, whose word was law to millions, and whose career has been closely chronicled and analysed. But he died powerless and dishonoured. He has no mausoleum of his own. He shares the one he built for his wife, his tomb installed as an afterthought. His name is forgettable.

The man's tomb is topped with a marble representation of a pen case, and the woman's, less clearly, with a representation of a slate. The message, which many women these days find unacceptable, is clear. However much Shah Jahan — that is the forgettable name — loved his wife Mumtaz he loved himself more, one of India's most perceptive historians has written. Surely he intended to honour his dead wife but not at the expense of his own reputation. The Taj Mahal is extraordinary not just in its splendid architecture but also in the story it has to tell.

It was observed of the famous Zophani [John Zoffany, a German who visited India in the 1780s], one of the most eminent painters of this age . . . . [that on seeing the Taj Mahal] he screamed out: Where is the case to cover so many beauties? For this is too fine to be exposed to the impression of the air. — Translated from an Indian writer's notes made at the time, published in India and British Portraiture, 1770-1825, by Mildred Archer, London, 1979. [No paintings made by Zoffany in India are known to have survived.]

This is generally presented as a love story but a friend's comment when I told her I planned this book is relevant. 'All I know is that I would not have wanted to be in Mumtaz's shoes or sandals for anything,' she said. 'Her entire life with Shah Jahan was spent having babies, seventeen or thereabouts, just one long, exhausting round of

pregnancies until she was completely worn out. What a love story!'

On the other hand, it is a story which has inspired so many romantic renderings that one loses count. There is no doubt about the love which existed between the emperor and his favourite wife, and her tragic ending makes their story still more emotional. If Shah Jahan is to be remembered at all, it is for his part in it. As an emperor, he was just another in the world's endless stream of powerful leaders; the Taj Mahal makes all the difference.

The way to see the Taj Mahal, then, is, slowly and if possible more than once. Not for nothing have generations of writers taking pen in hand conceded that this building is, well, indescribable, and then gone on at length to try to describe it. Dissenting views are few and usually contrived. Reading what travellers have had to say about the Taj Mahal often gets downright boring for their repetition of praise; but trying to learn for oneself what moved these commentators to such extremes of language is not in the least tedious. Give the Taj a chance and it will exert an influence on you that goes beyond words.

The indescribable charm of this building stems largely from its perpetually changing nature. The Taj at dawn is different from the Taj at noon or in the evening or beneath the light of the moon. It changes as clouds drift across the sun, and with the seasons as it registers the colours of the plains which extend to the horizon in every direction. One can barely comprehend that mere white marble, no matter how ingeniously worked, can display such variation until one has viewed the Taj under different conditions. In my own case, numerous visits produced not boredom but increasing fascination.

A few minutes in the course of a tiring day filled with numerous sights cannot do it justice. Stay at least one night in Agra, make an effort to see the Taj Mahal at dawn and return again at dusk. See it from afar as well as close up. Stroll about to see it from all possible angles. Sit in its excellent gardens and let its perfection work its way into your mind. Give it a chance. That is the way to see the Taj Mahal.

I will not attempt to describe the indescribable. Neither words nor pencil could give the most imaginative reader the slightest idea of the all-satisfying beauty and purity of this glorious conception. To those who have not seen it, I would say, 'Go to India. The Taj alone is worth the journey.' — Lord Roberts, an outstanding British soldier who was born in India and spent much of his career there.

Appreciating the Taj Mahal

Having made your way to Agra, and into the garden of the Taj Mahal, what do you find? What impression will the Taj have on you? A writer named John Keay took his wife there, and later wrote in a book (Into India, London, 1973) that he lost her in the crowd. 'When I found her,' he continued, 'She was standing quietly to one side apparently hypnotised. The only sign of life was a steady trickle of tears down each cheek.'

Mr Keay's wife is not alone in this reaction. You may experience it yourself or see it in others, and every teardrop flows down a channel well worn by history. More than a hundred years ago an Emma Roberts, writing descriptions to accompany drawings by a British navy officer named Robert Elliott, found that the Taj's 'melancholy sublimity' could touch and melt the heart. 'The eyes involuntarily gush out with tears; and many who have scarcely heard the name of her who sleeps within that honoured pile, approach the mausoleum weeping,' she wrote.

Not everyone is so deeply moved but those who know something of the story of the Taj are more likely to be. I listened in as a guide told a party of Australians, mostly women, about the building they had spent so much and come so far to see. 'The Taj Mahal was built by the Mughal Emperor Shah Jahan,' he said, 'as a mausoleum and

A photographer gets down to catch a Taj reflection. Many other visitors are content to look — and perhaps weep.

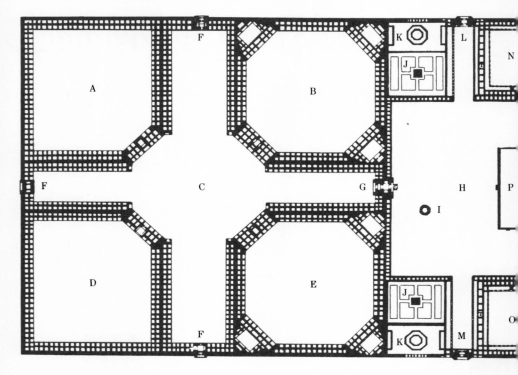

Thomas and William Daniell produced more than pictures of the Taje Mahel, as they spelt it. With their 1801 prints they published a booklet which included a brief description and this ground plan of the monument. It is reproduced here by permission of the Director, India Office Library and Records, the British Library.

More detailed and perhaps more accurate plans than this one by James Newton were to follow, but this serves as well as any to illustrate how the Taj Mahal is laid out.

More, it includes an idea of how the market area, on the extreme left, was arranged around a large courtyard. Today little of this market remains, except as walls built into the shops and houses of Tajganj.

The following key to the plan is based on James Newton's, with changes to create a sequence from left to right and with more recent information also included.

A. Market place for silks.
B. Omar Khan's market place.
C. Central market place.
D. Jugee Doj's market place.
E. Market place for scented oils.
F. Gates.
G. The south gate (which Newton called 'the lesser gate').
H. The great courtyard.

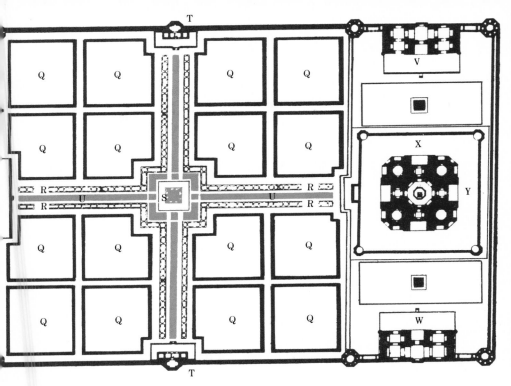

I. Well.
J. Raised gardens attached to tombs.
K. Tombs of 'Fattehporee' and 'Akbarabadee', two of Shah Jahan's wives. (More recent sources give different names.)
L. The west gate (which Newton called 'the principal gate').
M. The east gate.
N. Apartments for 'female attendants to ladies of rank' (now mostly empty; this enclosure is notable now for its garden, which is sometimes open to the public through a door in the main enclosure).
O. Apartments for female attendants (now a workshop and storage area).
P. The principal gate of the Taj Mahal.
Q. Gardens.
R. 'Paved walks through avenues of trees' and flower beds.
S. Large marble basin with fountains.
T. 'Summer houses' (one of which now houses the Taj Museum).
U. Channels for water with fountains.
V. The mosque.
W. 'A building corresponding in general form with V.'
X. 'A marble platform on which is erected the Taje Mahel.'
Y. 'The TAJE MAHEL.'

Newton's scale has been omitted as indecipherable; Taj Mahal dimensions are given on Page 36

Dimensions of the Taj Mahal

The walled enclosure within which the Taj Mahal stands is 562m x 302m (1843ft x 990ft), with an area of 17 hectares (42 acres).

The forecourt which leads to the main enclosure is 186m x 137m (610ft x 450ft), with an area of 2.5 hectares (6.1 acres).

The gateway building between the forecourt and the Taj Mahal enclosure is 45m wide x 35m high (150ft x 115ft) and the gateway itself is 11m wide x 20m high (37ft x 65ft).

Distance from the entrance platform to the central tank is 125m (412ft).

The water channels are 5m (16.5ft) wide.

The platform around the central tank is 22m (74.5ft) square.

Distance from the entrance platform to the mausoleum platform is 282m (925ft).

The enclosure where Mumtaz Mahal was temporarily buried is 5.8m x 5m (19ft x 16.5ft).

The platform on which the Taj Mahal stands is 95.5m (313ft) square.

The main building of the Taj Mahal is a square 56.5m (186ft) long on each side, with the corners cut off to create its octagonal shape.

Each side of the central octagonal chamber is 7.3m (24ft) long.

The sandstone platform which surrounds the main marble platform is 1.2m (4ft) above the general level of the garden.

The marble platform is 6.8m (22.5ft)

above the level of the garden.

The four minarets are 41.7m (137ft) high, and their tops are 49m (162ft) above the level of the garden.

The main walls of the Taj Mahal are almost 30m (100ft) high.

The inside height of the lower, inner dome — the one with the echo — is 24.4m (80ft).

The main dome on top of it is 17.6m (58ft) in diameter and 24.4m (80ft) high and its highest point is 65m (213ft) above the level of the garden.

The brass pinnacle, or finial, on top of the dome is 9.4m (31ft) high, and its tip is 74m (243ft) above garden level.

Floor plan of the main building.

memorial for his favourite wife, Mumtaz Mahal, after she died in Burhanpur, eight hundred kilometres from here, giving birth to their fourteenth child.'

There was a murmur of indrawn breath, a rustle of surprise, as if the visitors had not realised the building in front of them related to real people. They were not going to get a great deal from their visit. Later the same guide told me about an American woman who asked him, after a detailed tour of the Taj, when they would visit the Taj Mahal; she was worried it would not be airconditioned. And we talked to a couple who had seen the Eiffel Tower and the Parthenon and the Pyramids, and who thought the Taj Mahal was better than any of them.

There are some who come with a pretty fair idea that they are not going to like it much anyway. They may have read so much purple prose about it that they are surfeited; a normal reaction. In a sceptical, questioning age, they may have decided there must be more to the Taj Mahal story than the purely romantic version. And occasionally there is the thinking type who objects to anything which represents the exploitation of man by man, which means almost everything.

But the great majority of the thousands of visitors to the Taj are open to its influence, and an interesting time can be had watching people's faces as they come through the great main gate. Most remain impassive, some are distracted by their guides or companions, but some register wonder, delight, amazement. They are the fortunate ones, and they will never forget their visit.

Now, what is it that they see at the other end of that long garden? First impressions must involve size and symmetry. The Taj attains splendour partly through towering height and bulk, which lend stature to a design which would otherwise be coy and toylike. You have only to look at the alabaster models on sale throughout Agra to realise that anything smaller would be a failure.

The symmetry is apparent even at this stage. The lines of the garden paths and the central pond with its row of fountain nozzles converge on an entrance which stands precisely below the tip of the building's great dome. Later the visitor will find that the same precision applies to the placing of Mumtaz Mahal's tomb and even to the design of the marble screen around it. The only items in the entire complex not embraced in this splendid symmetry are Shah Jahan's tomb, which was an afterthought, and the remains of a small building where Mumtaz Mahal's body lay for years while waiting for its permanent resting place.

The mausoleum stands on a great marble platform, or podium, with minarets at each corner. The visitor who perceives these minarets to be not perfectly vertical perceives correctly, because they are designed to fall, if they fall, away from the main building. The mausoleum itself is square with the corners cut off, to create an octagonal shape.

Each corner is part of a smaller octagonal shape which is carried upwards as one of four linked towers which form, on their interior walls, a 'drum' which surrounds the central space and supports the great dome overhead, its top nearly sixtyfive metres above garden level. This can be compared with London's Nelson's Column, which is fiftytwo metres tall; or the eightyone metres of Washington's Capitol, or the fortyeight metres' gap between the deck of the Sydney Harbour Bridge and the water beneath. The Taj Mahal is not a monster but it is big enough to be seen clearly on the world stage.

A teardrop on the cheek of time.
— Rabindranath Tagore.

The main part of the Taj's dome is spherical, so that it appears to fit on to the drum like a ball in a cup, but it tapers slightly towards the top, where it takes the form of an inverted lotus flower. A metal finial, or crowning ornament, with Islamic and Hindu elements completes the towering effect. Four smaller domes top each of the four linked towers while narrow, vertical spikes from rooftop level keep the eye moving upwards. No rocket at Cape Canaveral was ever designed more precisely than the Taj Mahal to point the way to space. If a building alone can raise souls to heaven, that building is the Taj Mahal.

Like many visitors, I believed the Taj Mahal to be made of marble and confused my guide accordingly with questions he could not possibly answer. Later I learned that the marble (which is from Makrana, west of Jaipur in Rajasthan, four hundred and twenty kilometres away) is a veneer a few centimetres thick over a core made of bricks and mortar. Visitors can confirm this by poking around in the northwest corner of the garden, where marble removed from the Taj for whatever reason is stored before being taken away. It is in slabs, not blocks. Learning this was vaguely disappointing because marble is more romantic than bricks and veneer smacks of cheapness; but the Taj could not have been built in any other way, and admiration returned.

I can truly say that everything surpassed my expectations. I at first thought the dome formed too large a portion of the whole building; that the neck was too long and too much exposed; and that the minarets were too plain in their design; but after going repeatedly over every part, and examining the tout ensemble from all possible positions, and in all possible lights, from that of the full moon at midnight in a cloudless sky, to that of the noon-day sun, the mind seemed to repose in the calm persuasion that there was an entire harmony of parts, a faultless congregation of architectural beauties, on which it could dwell for ever without fatigue. . . . One returns and returns to it with undiminished pleasure. — W.H. Sleeman (husband of the woman who said she would 'die tomorrow' to be buried under such a building, in Rambles and Recollections of an Indian Official, 1844, writing about a visit in 1836.

It is the most divine creation of a building in the whole world. You will never be able to satisfy your eyes by seeing it enough. — Mary Curzon, wife of Lord Curzon, Viceroy of India, about 1900.

A different emotion came into play when an elegant hostess in Delhi showed me a sliver of white marble and said it was from the Taj Mahal. What was going on? The explanation turned out to be innocent. She had seen a workman repairing broken marble, had asked him what he would do with the pieces, and was told they would be thrown away. So she asked for one, and is proud of it. Suggestions that India could pay off its national debt by selling such fragments, however, were quickly put down. There would be no way of knowing which came from the Taj and which had been newly carved from the ground in Makrana, where the quarries are still producing.

Were the Taj purely white, it would not be as impressive as it is. The difference lies in the stone inlay work which has been used to embellish the exterior. Verses from the Koran surround

This cutaway drawing shows the structure of the double dome and position of the lower burial chamber.

the main arches and floral patterns adorn the base of the dome and spaces which would otherwise appear overly blank. But it is all very subtle, doing nothing to detract from the building's overall dignity. The Mughals built like titans and finished like jewellers, commented an early European traveller.

Inside, where you walk in bare feet or with cloth slippers over your shoes to protect the marble flooring, more surprises await, one huge, others so fine you almost need a magnifying glass to appreciate them. The huge surprise is another dome, within the one you see from outside. Mughal builders had earlier learned that double domes provided an answer to the need for strength within and height without, and the Taj Mahal makes expert use of their knowledge. The dome over the tomb replicas is twentyfour metres high, high enough to produce a splendid echo.

In the literature about the Taj, so often repeated that I cannot trace its origin, is this comment: 'The echo floats and soars overhead in a long and delicious undulation, fading away so slowly that you hear it after it is silent.' I watched as visitors tried to time the echo, only to be frustrated by being unable to detect when sound ended and silence began. At times guides' spiels — 'Within this building is laid to rest the immortal Mumtaz Mahal. . . .' — can resonate around the chamber like a sermon.

The secret of the beauty of the Taj Mahal lies in the great arched recesses which burrow deep into the body of the building. These are throbbing with sensitive shadows, and they give the impression that the onlooker can see into the very heart of this gentle palace as one would gaze into the heart of a yellow rose, where, leaf by leaf, the tints become deeper, warmer and move living. There is ever a sense of something half hidden and half revealed, of a tenderness that has deeper depths, of a beauty which is but partly shown, of a bosom shadowed by white lace. It is this abiding suggestion that makes the peculiar glory of the Taj, a glory which is beyond the reach of any model or any picture. To many the Taj will ever be the most beautiful building in the world, while there must be few who will not acknowledge that it is the most lovable monument that has ever been erected over the dead. — Sir Frederick Treves, in The Other Side of the Lantern, London, 1905.

An 1896 guidebook warned of a different problem: 'Visitors who play complicated melodies or roulades [in the chamber] will be disappointed. The echo is so quick that it catches the notes and runs them into one another so as to produce a most distressing discord, unless the notes are chosen to produce a natural harmony. The chord of the seventh produces a very beautiful effect.'

Then there are the tombs themselves. Unless one believes apocryphal stories about actual graves being on a lower level still, Mumtaz Mahal and Shah Jahan are buried beneath the floor of a gloomy, mainly undecorated room reached by descending twenty-four steep steps from the building's main chamber. Often the number of people going down that stairway is so great that the unventilated

room becomes airless and stifling. But it is worth accepting the discomfort in exchange for a close look at the two tombs.

Both here and in the more spacious chamber above where replicas of the tombs stand, precisely above the lower ones to prevent people walking over them, the quality of the inlay work is extraordinary. Semi-precious stones have been set into the white marble in such quantity and so precisely that the result seems almost alive. As many as sixty tiny slivers of different gemstones can go into a single flower, and there are so many flowers of so many kinds that an

inventory of this garden — if that is the right word — is almost impossible.

The stones used include turquoise, jade, agate, coral, lapis lazuli, onyx, bloodstone, cornelian, jasper, garnet and malachite, and the flowers they have been shaped into include fuchsias, lilies, tiger lilies, honeysuckle, poppies and a variety which the guides call grape, but which I could not recognise. It has been commented that the flowers are all alien to central India and represent a Mughal harking back to the cooler climates of Kashmir and central Asia. The four tombs also carry quotations from the Koran, all inlaid in immaculate calligraphy.

Symmetry extends even to the division of the marble screen, left, into equal parts. Such screenwork softens the light around the two tombs, above. Note the illicit candles.

Mumtaz Mahal's tombs, both upper and lower, identify her in the same terms: 'Here lies Arjumand Banu Begum, called Mumtaz Mahal, who died in 1040 Hijrah (AD 1630/31).' On Shah Jahan's tomb in the upper chamber are inscribed the words: 'Here lies Shah Jahan, Emperor, called Firdaus Ashyani [dweller in paradise], who was born like Timur when Jupiter and Venus were in the same constellation in heaven. He died in 1076 Hijrah (AD 1665/66).'

The inscription on Shah Jahan's tomb in the lower chamber is longer. It reads: 'The illuminated and sacred resting place of Shah Jahan, Emperor, dignified as Razwan, having his abode in paradise and his dwelling in the starry heavens, called Firdaus Ashyani [dweller in paradise], who was born like Timur when Jupiter and Venus were in the same constellation and who was a valiant ruler. His mausoleum shall ever flourish and his abode shall be in heaven. He left this transitory world for the world of eternity on the night of 28 Rajab 1076 Hijrah (AD 1665/66).'

The caretakers and the guides are willing sources of much information but not all of it is reliable. 'Guides?' snorted a government official when I tried to check an outlandish story one had given me. 'They are misguides!' One pointed out a space on Shah Jahan's real tomb and said that it had once been occupied by the Kohinoor dia-

Bullock-powered mowers keep the Taj lawns in trim.

mond, now in Queen Elizabeth's crown. It may once have been in Shah Jahan's treasury — but it was never in the Taj Mahal.

Not only the tombs are inlaid, and more finely and to a greater depth than the inlaid marble tabletops and trinkets which many tourists take home from Agra. The tombs in the upper chamber are surrounded by a carved marble screen almost two metres high which carries a wealth of flowers made from gems. The screen (said to have replaced an earlier one made of gold) is ornamental in its own right and lends much also to the ambience of the chamber, filtering light to an engaging softness. Were it protected from visitors' hands, instead of being dark with their sweat and grease, it would be still more charming. One day, according to Archaeological Survey of India (ASI) proposals, it will be, but it is a step which a people-minded administration is reluctant to take.

However, a listing of the Taj Mahal's component marvels does not do the building justice. It is greater than the sum of its parts. To consider only its pieces would be like thinking of a fine painting only in terms of its canvas and different pigments, or a sculpture in terms of its chemical composition. Appreciating the Taj means letting all its components fall naturally into place in your mind. This takes time, and the best place to pass such time is in the Taj garden.

I could not have believed there could be anything like it. A massive marble structure without weight, as if composed of ether; perfectly rational and yet purely decorative; without ascertainable content, and yet full of significance in the highest degree: the Taj Mahal is not only one of the greatest works of art, it is perhaps the greatest of all pieces of artifice which the creative spirit of man has ever achieved. — Hermann Keyserling, a German philosopher, in The Travel Diary of a Philosopher, 1925.

The garden of the Taj Mahal is inseparable from the Taj Mahal because they derive from parallel traditions. The mausoleum continued a line of development which will be traced later, and the garden results from a tradition reaching back to central Asia.

Long before the Mughals (originally, Mongols) came into India, they devised a unique approach to garden design based on the division of the total area into four equal parts. The idea was literally to create an image of paradise on earth; the word 'paradise' derives from the old Persian 'pairidaeza', which means an enclosed garden. A Koranic inscription on the main gateway to the Taj Mahal, continuing this concept, is an invitation to consider the Creator, and to enter His garden as one of His servants.

In one important aspect, however, the Taj garden broke with the Mughal tradition. Instead of being in the centre of the garden, the mausoleum is at one end, giving it the advantages both of a long perspective from the main gate and a towering position over the Yamuna river. These seem to be reasons enough, but the switch from tradition was so marked that it invited further scrutiny. This in turn led directly to the myth of the Taj Mahal's black marble counterpart across the river.

Seeking reasons for the change, Nineteenth Century archaeologists speculated that perhaps Shah Jahan planned to restore symmetry by building another mausoleum on the north bank of the Yamuna, which he himself would one day occupy. That was enough to inspire further conjecture.

Others found significance in the fact that Shah Jahan had not otherwise prepared his own mausoleum, and saw some ruins on the north bank as evidence that work had actually begun. As a result visitors today are almost routinely told that there was to have been a black marble Taj facing Mumtaz Mahal's white one, and even that there was to be a bridge of silver connecting the two.

. . . . You saunter through a glorious garden of flowers and foliage unconscious of what awaits you. . . . Arrived at the top, why do you stand in breathless astonishment, your feet rivetted to the spot? Ah, why indeed? To that question I can give no satisfactory answer: I can only say the Taj stands before you. — Samuel Bourne, a pioneering photographer of Indian monuments.

The story persists though there is not a word of evidence in the Mughal annals to support it, and though those ruins on the north bank almost certainly derive from an earlier period. So entrenched is the idea of a black marble counterpart to the white one, both in folk lore and now in writing as well, that it will probably never die. Few people pause to consider that Shah Jahan, a man who had many failings but fine architectural judgement, would probably have considered such a proposal at least crass, probably grotesque. The Taj Mahal is sited where it is, at the end of the garden, because that is the best place for it.

And the garden is the best place from which to view and think about the Taj Mahal. This has not always been so. In its original version, as an earthly paradise, the garden was much boskier than it is

From across the Yamuna river, the Taj Mahal appears to float above a field of flowering mustard.

today, especially with fruit trees. There exists an old contract wherein one Ahmad Zaman was given the right to harvest fruit in the Taj garden for one year, from September 1800 to August 1801.

Old paintings and even early photographs of the Taj Mahal show trees encroaching much more closely then they do today on to the central pathway and watercourse. None of the original trees has survived. There were no lawns, because the grasses which make good lawns were not available in India in those days and because lawnmowers had not been invented; picnickers would have taken along carpets to sit on. Today's lawns are soft and pleasant, kept in trim by bullock-powered mowers whose drivers are liable to stop and smile whenever they see a camera pointing their way.

Cameras are very much part of the Taj scene. Every other visitor seems to have one. A student of cameras would be in his element because they are of all types from all over the world. More, they are kept busy. A statistically minded person who spent a day counting cameras and estimating how often each one was used, and then tried to compute how many pictures are taken in the Taj garden each year would arrive at something astronomical.

For people who do not bring cameras there are the resident professionals, fifty of them licensed, many more not, who will take your picture against the Taj for a small fee — three-quarters down and the rest when your picture arrives COD, anywhere in India. They average ten or fifteen customers a day, are delighted with twenty and get depressed with only four or five. When not busy they tend to be boisterous.

All tourists take pictures of the Taj Mahal. A few also use the opportunity to photograph birds, here gathered handily into a neat area and not all that shy of people. An ornithologist's checklist could include the following: Doves, pigeons, parakeets, nightjars, swifts, sparrows, hoopoes, larks, wagtails, bulbuls, flycatchers, mynas, fantails, babblers, Indian robins and munias. And that is not counting the crows, kites, hawks, eagles and vultures overhead and the waders in the shallow waters of the Yamuna. One day someone will do a book on the birds of the Taj.

Among the people who helped with information for this book was Mr S.N. Singh, a former chief horticulturist to the ASI, whose office was in Agra, just outside the Taj Mahal garden, and who still lives there. He told how this century in particular has seen a gradual transforma-

Downstream offers more fine views — and village children as well.

tion in the design of the garden. While the original basic layout has been retained, old trees have been replaced as they died with shadier and more fragrant ones, especially around the periphery. Vistas have been opened up, not just towards the Taj but also to the other buildings on each side. Pruning the trees to maintain this openness is a regular feature of garden maintenance.

'Much attention has also been paid to colour schemes,' he said.

'My predecessor at one stage bedded the whole central strip with pansies and roses. The result was so spectacular that people were distracted from the Taj. When I took over I moved the flower plots back from the central strip and made them smaller, and changed back to flowers with softer colours. Now there is no distraction from the central attraction.' The Taj's gardeners work to three seasons, winter, summer and rainy, and change the flowers three times a year. When we were there they were mainly petunias and calendulas, with some florence roses, cannas and lilies.

Mr Singh is better remembered among the Taj's workers and officials, however, as the man who got the fountains working again. They had not worked for decades and previous attempts to solve the pro-

The fountains, brought back to life, add to the charm of the gardens. it is unfortunate they do not play more often.

blem had failed, once because too much water pressure was applied to the ancient Mughal system. This system involved a canal from the Yamuna river into a compound outside the west wall and bullock-powered lifting devices such as one still finds in the villages. Water raised by this means was stored in an overhead cistern with more than one hundred and eighty thousand litres capacity which was divided into three sections. While water flowed down to the fountains

---

The building I am speaking of is of a different and peculiar kind [from those of the same class in France]; but not without something pleasing in its whimsical structure; and in my opinion it well deserves a place in our books of architecture. It consists almost wholly of arches upon arches, and galleries upon galleries, disposed and contrived in a hundred different ways. Nevertheless the edifice has a magnificent appearance, and is conceived and executed ef-fectively. Nothing offends the eye; on the contrary, it is delighted with every part, and never tired with looking. . . . This monument deserves much more to be numbered among the wonders of the world than the pyramids of Egypt, those unshapen masses which when I had seen them twice yielded me no satisfaction. — Francois Bernier, Travels in the Mogul Empire, 1670. (Bernier was a physician in Emperor Aurangzeb's court for many years.)

---

from one of these sections, used water was returned to one of the other sections, ready to be used again. It was all very ingenious.

When Mr Singh was handed the problem of getting the derelict system working again, about 1960, he sank three wells and installed pumps to keep the cistern filled — and found that the original Mughal method was as good as ever. The BBC broadcast a feature about 'the Taj springing back to life' and Mr Singh got a letter of appreciation from the Prime Minister.

Nonetheless, a visitor today will be lucky to see the fountains working. Though Mr Singh says the system is self-contained, producing its own water, the official line is that fountain playing is restricted — which usually means to official visits — because of a shortage of water. The real reason could be that before the fountains are turned on someone has to screw special nozzles into eightyfour fountain heads; and after the show he has to go round and take them out again before they are stolen.

This diffidence is unfortunate because the fountains make the

attractive gardens better. More, said Mr Singh, playing the fountains would permit a still more remarkable change. 'We knew the Mughals were very fond of aromatic flowers, so we added rosewater and rose scent to the overhead cistern. When the fountains played, the whole garden was perfumed.'

Other buildings in the Taj Mahal grounds include a mosque in the northwest corner, with praying places for more than five hundred worshippers inlaid carpet-like into the floor. Then there is a replica of the mosque in the northeast corner which serves no purpose except to maintain symmetry; it is known as the Jawab, a word meaning response or answer. Two halfway houses, as it were, are set into the surrounding walls on each side half way along.

One of these, the one on the left, is used as a museum and offers a small but interesting collection of Taj-related items. They include paintings, seals, weapons and other memorabilia from Shah Jahan's times, specimens of inlay work, calligraphy and old coins, and an old site plan of the Taj Mahal, blackened with age, which identifies even the fruit trees planted in the garden.

There are also copies of orders from Shah Jahan to the ruler in Jaipur, in Rajasthan, concerning the supply of marble from the quarries at Makrana. One deals with the wages to be paid to workers mining and transporting the marble, another with the supply of wagons, and a third with the need for stone-cutters to be taken off other jobs and sent to Makrana. A booklet about the museum published by the ASI includes an excellent brief history of the Taj Mahal.

There is one more building, or the remains of a building, in the Taj grounds, small and often overlooked. A simple, stone enclosure, originally domed but now without a roof, it is where Mumtaz Mahal's body was buried in December, 1631, after its arrival from Burhanpur, where she died the previous June. This was her grave while the Taj Mahal took shape nearby. Eventually her remains would be transferred to their present resting place, and years later, in 1666, Shah Jahan's body would be laid beside her.

Friday prayers in the Taj Mahal mosque.

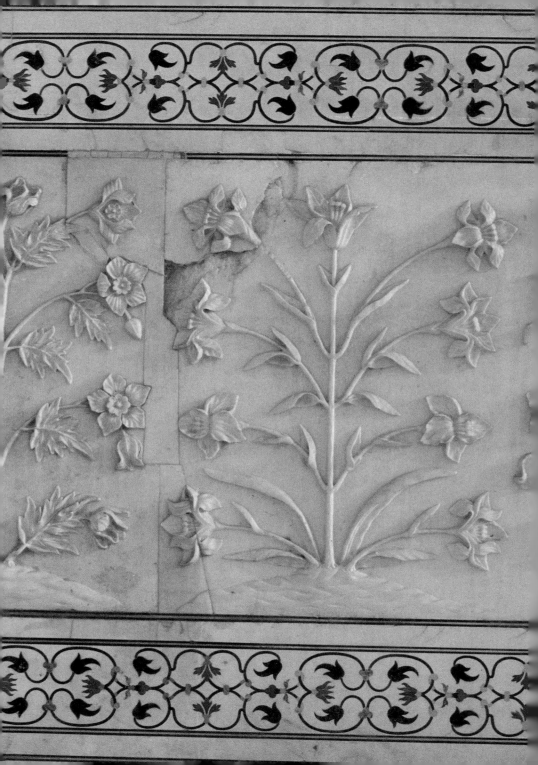

Conditions may have changed recently, but when we were working on this book senior officials in the ASI seemed reluctant to intervene. Trouble within the Taj Mahal was the last thing they wanted. Their concerns were more with conservation of the entire building and with ways to manage ever increasing numbers of visitors. Attempts to impose discipline, unless cleverly done, could too easily boil up into a public row over whether procedures hallowed by tradition could so easily be discarded.

Instead of the spacious squares and frequented streets of a great capital, it was with difficulty and danger we kept our horses on their feet amidst the magnificent but terrible mass of ruin. Few persons can have an idea of the painful sensations excited by such a view of this once celebrated city. . . . In the midst of this chaotic heap of desolation, our attention was suddenly roused by a stupendous fabric bursting on our view, in complete repair and resplendent beauty — a splendid structure, with domes and minarets of the purest white, surmounting the dark umbrage of rich surrounding groves, produced in such a situation a most extraordinary effect. — James Forbes, in Oriental Memoirs, London, 1813, describing a visit some years earlier.

The ASI could do without such complications because it was already under enough pressure from recurring stories that the Taj Mahal was falling down or being dangerously corroded by pollution. All its senior officers are familiar with scare headlines that set their phones ringing — the Taj is always news, and the scarier the better. They are also familiar with the truth, which is much less dramatic and therefore much harder to put across.

'There are these reports that crop up from time to time about cracks in the Taj, as if they were new and as if they mean that the building is falling down,' an ASI engineer told me. 'But all buildings have cracks. Having cracks means nothing — you have to say what sort of cracks. In the Taj Mahal, they are superficial, in the marble. They occur mainly because the iron dowels holding the marble to the brick core are rusting, and rust takes more room then iron does; the expansion can cause cracking. The interior core of bricks and mortar is solid, and so are the foundations. There is no threat to the stability of the monument.'

The bricks and mortar core is so solid, another archaeologist told me, 'that no modern chisel can break the bricks apart'. The formula for that mortar reads like a cooking recipe. Slaked lime and powdered bricks are basic ingredients, and there is also raw sugar, lentils, flour and vegetable gum: you could almost eat it like a kind of muesli. The formula is still used for repair work on the Taj Mahal and other old buildings around Agra.

And repair work has been going on for a long time. As long ago as 1652 Shah Jahan's son Aurangzeb wrote a letter to him reporting leaks in the Taj's dome and cracks in some of the chambers — in a building completed less than ten years before. Reports for the next

century or so are scanty, but late in the 18th Century a traveller could report that in 1789 the Taj was in very good repair — only to suffer damage by lightning a year later. 'The cullice [?] which decorated the top of the principal dome was struck down,' he reported, 'and the dome at the same time received material injury.' It was to be feared, he continued, that the building might find no master to restore and preserve it.

A few years later, in 1803, a kind of master came marching in. The British, who had been spreading through India for more than a century, took Agra. They made themselves secure in the old Mughal Fort, looked around, realised that the Taj Mahal was special — and set up

Ruins all around — but the Taj Mahal remained safe.

a committee to look after it. A British officer, a Captain Taylor, was assigned to cleaning and repairing the whole building, a herculean assignment.

There are pretty reliable reports that up to this time the finial atop the main dome had been coated with gold but that thereafter it was made of brass. The one now installed is reported to be about nine metres high while an outline of it in stone at ground level, near the Jawab in the northeast corner of the grounds, to give visitors an idea of its size is about eight and half metres long. The difference is prob-

---

On approaching the famous city of Agra, or Akbar-abad, the most melancholy remains of former grandeur presented themselves on all sides: mosques, palaces, gardens, caravanserais and mausoleums, mingled in one general ruin! On entering the gate of the city, at which there was no guard, I proceeded through a quarter called Mumtazabad, over a chaos of desolation for about two miles, to Taje Mahl, the gem or diadem of the seraglio, which was the place allotted . . . . for my accommodation. . . . This building, in point of design and execution, is one of the most extensive, elegant, commodious and perfect works ever undertaken and finished by one man [an architect to whom Shah Jahan gave the title of Zerreer Dust, or Jewel-Handed]. . . . The astonishing art and niceness of the masonry has hitherto admirably withstood the devastations of time; nor has a succession of barbarous and predatory invaders yet dared to violate the sanctity and beauty of this wonderful fabric.' — Sir Charles Malet, about 1794.

---

ably entirely without significance.

The Taj Mahal faced further threats during the Indian Mutiny, or War of Independence, depending whose versions you read, which broke out in 1857. As the revolt spread the British in Agra and their supporters were forced to retreat into the Fort. The Cantonment area was plundered and mansions which had lined the river bank between the Taj Mahal and the Fort were mostly destroyed — making way for today's parks. But the awe which the Taj induces in many visitors continued to work its magic and it was not damaged. The British spent several months in the Fort before being rescued, apparently not in great discomfort. A report published in London said that 'the exuberance of their mirth' was so great the commander issued an order 'condemnatory of singing and playing of flutes and cornopeans'.

In 1874 work on the Taj Mahal by the Public Works Department included repairs to the finial, treatment of the main dome with portland cement, and the re-erection of some fallen pinnacles on the main gate. Electric lights were installed in 1876 and later some ramshackle buildings were cleared away.

And so on, with some famous names, particularly those of Lord Strachey, a lieutenant governor of the Northwest Provinces, and later Lord Curzon, a viceroy of India, appearing as protectors of the Taj Mahal. Curzon, who founded the ASI, took a special interest in the Agra monument, supplying the great lamp in the main tomb chamber (replacing one which had been stolen) and generally refurbishing it. 'If I had never done anything else in India, I have written my name here, and the letters are a living joy,' he wrote.

Lord Curzon

Here is Curzon's summary of what he achieved: 'The Taj itself and its surroundings are now all but free of the workmen's hands. It is no longer approached through dusty wastes and a squalid bazaar. A beautiful park takes their place; and the group of mosques and tombs, the arcaded streets and grassy courts that precede the main building are once more as nearly as possible what they were when completed by the masons of Shah Jahan. Every building in the garden enclosure of the Taj has been scrupulously repaired, and the discovery of old plans has enabled us to restore the water channels and flowerbeds of the garden more exactly to their original state.'

On the other hand, there was need of such ministrations. The Taj Mahal, though admired, had not attained among the British the hallowed respect it enjoys today. It was the victim of much casual and potentially damaging treatment. The marble platform was used for concerts. Honeymooners camped in the Jawab or in the garden. There are reports of young British officers, after languid lunches, prowling around trying to prise out inlay-work gems with their swords. The building and grounds were open to all.

More seriously, there had been at least one proposal to strip the Taj Mahal of its best marble work. In the 1830s, Lord William Bentinck, a newly appointed governor-general, casting about for ways to rescue his administration from financial danger, organised the auction of a considerable number of marble pieces from the Agra Fort. If the sale had gone well, the Taj itself would have been looted. But, according to writer John Lall, Indian merchants united solidly to ensure that the auction was a failure. The Taj was saved.

Countless visitors to Agra are told versions of this story, and are suitably appalled. 'Disgraceful,' they mutter. In fairness to Bentinck, it should be added that he was one of the most enlightened of Britain's administrators in India. He reformed education and judicial processes, suppressed human sacrifice and the murder of unwanted children, and — a detail equally to impress those shocked tourists — abolished sati, the custom whereby widows were burned to death on their husbands' funeral pyres. Or rather, he made it illegal and did what he could to enforce the law, as has every administration since.

So here we have Emma Roberts once more, earlier quoted as writing that so many visitors involuntarily found their eyes gushing with tears: 'The British government has with laudable zeal taken the Taje Mahal under its especial protection; more than twelve thousand pounds have been expended on its repairs, the garden is kept in perfect order, and the whole is always open to European and native visitors. The latter take a great and natural pride in this superb memorial of former power. Upon a Sunday evening, when the fountains are playing, the garden exhibits gay groups of shewy figures, variously attired, some with caftans of velvet, or brocade, bordered with gold; others, more gaudy, shining out in tinsel finery; and a plainer description clad in white garments, bound round with flowing shawls; while the very poorest classes crowd from the neighbouring city to this favourite spot . . .'

The Taj is incomparable, designed like a palace and finished like a jewel. . . . pure, perfect and unutterably lovely. One feels the same sensation as in gazing at a beautiful woman, one who has that mixture of loveliness and sadness which is essential to the highest beauty. — Lord Curzon, Viceroy of India, about 1900.

In recent decades preservation of the Taj Mahal has become more systematic. 'Committees of experts' have existed for at least fifty years to ensure that conservation work is sensible and consistent. The ASI's annual reports show that year by year broken stonework and damaged inlays were repaired, drainage improved, the gardens developed, administration tightened. There were no dramatic episodes. Everything was under control, and perhaps everybody concerned became a little lax.

The people of Agra had long been accustomed to the Taj Mahal's gates remaining open, to the gardens being free to all comers by night and day, and to occasional festivals in the Taj grounds, particularly on the night of the full moon. An annual full moon festival, by the name of Sharad Purnima, was famous far beyond Agra and sometimes attracted more than twenty thousand people.

Against this background, several years ago, word spread that a film company planned to shoot scenes in the Taj grounds, and that a heart-throb actor named Dilip Kumar would be involved. An unruly crowd of fans resulted, with much littering and damage to the gardens. By chance a government minister from Delhi was present, and his anger led to two important changes in the way the Taj is run.

First, there would be no more film-making in the grounds; any producer intent on using the Taj in his scenes must use a plywood and plaster model or make do with long views from outside the walls. We went looking for a vantage point outside for long shots, and were taken through a narrow lane, through a private house, up a stairway, through a bedroom and up a bamboo ladder to a tiny patch of roof just south of the Taj. 'This is where the James Bond film people shot the Taj Mahal scene for Octopussy,' we were told. 'They weren't allowed into the grounds.' We could not find anyone who remembered if Octopussy had a Taj scene or not.

Second, the Indian central government in Delhi decided the time had come for the ASI to impose an admission charge. As stated earlier, today this charge has grown to a still minute two rupees, one quarter of it for the ASI and three quarters for the Agra Development Authority, about which more later. Children are admitted free and there is no charge on Fridays, when many Muslims attend prayers at the mosque in the Taj grounds. On these days as many as twenty thousand people may turn up, against a daily average around five thousand.

These changes brought a certain discipline to the business of running the Taj Mahal, and certainly helped keep the gardens in order. Everything settled down once more, until the 1980s when the care and conduct of Taj affairs began to claim unusual space in Indian headlines and editorial columns.

Hafeez Ahmed, apparently relaxed in the grounds of the Taj Mahal, is actually hard at work keeping alive generations of family history. He has no doubt that he is descended from a family which left Lahore more than three hundred years ago to help build Mumtaz Mahal's memorial. They were specialists in marble work even then, and today Mr Hafeez is one of a select group of inlay designers.

He goes to the Taj to seek inspiration, draws his patterns, and goes back to his workshop to turn them into stone. More, he brings to his work an especially close link with the Taj Mahal — in the 1960s he spent eighteen months working inside, replacing stones which had been prised out in more casual times.

Just as marble inlay work is one of the glories of the Taj, so it is the liveliest of all handcraft industries in Agra today. Thousands of boys and men (but virtually no women) are involved in carving marble, shaping slivers of semi-precious stone, and bringing the two together often to spectacular effect. Entering a showroom full of inlaid marble for the first time can be a stunning experience. Tabletops are the most expensive  items and many tourists settle for lesser items such as coasters, ashtrays or small decorative panels.

Mr Hafeez has been through the inlay mill. He began work at the age of fourteen and has been at it ever since, these days with no fewer than forty other members of his extended family. He was

69

fiftyfour when this picture was taken, and he expected to keep going for a few more years — eyesight permitting. 'Many of us get weak eyes from all that close work and from poor lighting,' he said. He has callouses on the outside of his feet from decades spent sitting crosslegged.

The work is hard and at the same time incredibly finicky. Shaping and polishing the slabs of marble from Makrana in Rajasthan is laborious. Carving out the runnels and flats where the semi-precious stones will be inserted demands such pressure on the steel chisel that workers develop permanent grooves in the tips of their index fingers. The patterns they must follow are scratched as white lines in a brown dye on the surface of the marble. The dye is later removed.

Shaping the stones which will be laid into the marble is an entirely different skill. Many tiny bits may go into one ornamental shape, perhaps thousands into a finished tabletop, and each must be held to a revolving emery wheel until it is precisely right.

Stones traditionally used include lapis lazuli, cornelian, jasper, garnet, jade, malachite, agate, tiger's eye, coral and turquoise. When all is ready, a traditional cement kept hot by burning charcoal is inserted into the marble and the stone sections are gingerly put in place on top. When the cement cools the connection is permanent.

Salesmen delight in saying how tough the final product is, and in pouring drinks over it to show the marble will never stain. One insisted you could turn an inlaid tabletop upside down and use the rougher surface as a chopping board without risk to the fine work on the other side. Certainly the marble has a crystalline whiteness not often seen; it is said to be the hardest in the world.

All inlay workers in Agra are

Muslim (though the marble cutters may be Hindu), and this is said to be both traditional and a restraint on the scope of the industry. The tradition may be more recent than the building of the Taj Mahal because E.B. Havell has reported that five named for their work on the Taj all had Hindu names. The restraint arises from the limitation it places on the number of young men willing to become inlay workers.

Young men, not young women. In this field as in others in India women are not welcome, though they could undoubtedly do as well as men, probably better. The reason is simple. 'Girls marry into other families,' said Mr Hafeez. 'We don't teach them because when they marry they would take the skill away with them.'

Mr Ashok Jain, who has been in the inlay business since 1972 (and whose workers use Mr Hafeez's designs), said that the marble used had to be spotless, lineless and milky white; only about five percent from the Makrana quarries met these stipulations. As for the stones inlaid in the marble, these are the same as in Mughal times except that sodalite at times replaces lapis lazuli and irridescent New Zealand paua shell is used in

some new designs. About three-quarters of the stone is lost in the process of shaping.

The best inlay work now is of high quality. Rising tourist numbers have created a demand for fine work which the industry has been able to meet (while also

me.' Foreign tourists account for almost ninety percent of all sales; oddly, Indian marble inlay work is not popular in India.

However, though the quality has improved in recent years, it will never regain the excellence that went into the inlay work on

turning out the cheap stuff offered on street corners, often using Italian alabaster instead of marble). Mr Ashok said the larger market permits better materials to be used and more quality control to be applied.

He has two inspectors who do nothing but examine work in progress, which is almost always in workers' homes. There are no factories, nor is it possible to fill the occasional orders from overseas stores which want large numbers of identical items. At least, not without sacrificing quality. 'Some other producers will do it,' Mr Ashok said. 'Not

the Taj Mahal tombs. The reason is simple. In Shah Jahan's day expense was never questioned and the stones inlaid into the marble were often substantial, set into deep grooves. These days costs must be closely watched — so the stones are sliced into sections only two millimetres thick. People used to prise stones from the Taj Mahal because they were worth having; trying to get them from a modern tabletop would be a waste of time.

Not all marble work involves inlaying. The Taj Mahal has superb panels and screens — and

the tradition has not been lost.
Work in marble continues in
Agra, especially at Dayalbagh,
about five kilometres north of the
town centre.

Here construction began in
1904 on a temple which will serve
as headquarters of the
Radhasoami faith, which was
founded last century by Soamiji
Maharaj. Apart from a break
between 1911 and 1922, work has
been going on ever since, 'stone
upon stone and brick upon brick
in patient humility'. Pillars and
walls towered high overhead when
this book was written but the
temple was still far from comple-
tion.

Enough had been achieved,
however, to show that the art of

working marble like Plasticine is
not dead. Pillars are adorned with
precisely wrought fruit, flowers
and foliage, not only in white
Makrana marble but also in pink
and green stone as well. Work goes
ahead slowly, with men in the
surrounding yard carving huge
slabs of marble into shape and
others hauling finished pieces
into position.

The completed temple will be
exceedingly ornate, will
incorporate a towering bulbous
dome, and will be nearly sixty
metres high. Much solid marble
will be included, especially in
supporting columns, and there
will be brickwork as well faced
with marble slabs — just as in the
Taj Mahal.

The Eighties — a decade of change

The Taj Mahal is always news in India, and recent events have kept it in the headlines. Sometimes it seems unfair because the Archaeological Survey of India does a good job of running it. The ASI, which looks after more than three thousand five hundred monuments throughout India, including a hundred with 'priority attention' status, has a contained and low-key approach to management which works well. But Indian politicians and journalists need convenient footballs to kick just as much as do their counterparts in other countries. Since the Taj Mahal is so well known and since the ASI rarely kicks back, critical comment is easy. Even without this, however, there was bound to be action when three distinct forces came to impinge on that famous building in Agra.

First, tourism, which had long been regarded as a kind of minor cultural distraction, broke through into real economics as a potential source of much more money than it had been generating. The promotion of India became important — and what better to help promote India than images of the Taj Mahal? Suddenly it became not only one of the country's most important cultural assets, but a major economic one as well.

Second, following from the first, there came greater interest in the Taj's well-being — just at a time when it was visibly suffering from

Alabaster models of the Taj Mahal sell well, along with all manner of other souvenirs, mostly kitsch.

another great developmment, industrialisation and pollution across the plains of northern India. Keeping the Taj white and pristine became a matter of national importance. Plans for a big oil refinery at Mathura, only forty kilometres and reputedly upwind from Agra, fuelled the issue.

And third, to make a serious issue critical, terrorists found that a sure way to alarm the government was to threaten to destroy the Taj. The protection of this monument suddenly achieved a new and more demanding meaning. The potential enemy was not just slow-working smog but a cunningly planted bomb. It would need to be a big bomb

A newspaper version of what could happen.

indeed seriously to damage the big and solid Taj Mahal but even a minor blast would have loud political echoes.

When officials in Delhi put all this together, there must have been times when the Taj, two hundred kilometres away, loomed so large in their lives that they felt they could see it on the horizon. When the Prime Minister's office became directly involved, senior ASI men knew that their days when they could concentrate on academic and research issues were gone for ever. Rarely can archaeologists, who presumably like quiet lives, have been thrust so abruptly to centre stage.

The change which had been building up slowly accelerated in May, 1984, when Usha Rai, a Times of India journalist, received a report on the Taj Mahal from a government building research laboratory in Bhopal, compiled by three Indian scientists and one American, a materials engineering specialist from California.

The result was a report in the Times which was headed, 'Taj must be saved . . . and now,' and which said that large, deep cracks up to ten feet long and a few millimetres wide had appeared both inside and outside the Taj Mahal. In some places small pieces of marble had begun falling out, it added, while 'a sickly yellow pallor' pervaded the inside of the monument. In places yellow patches were magnified by ugly brown and black spots. In the lower tomb chamber burning candles 'cast an eerie glow on the blackened, fungus-eaten marble'. The building was infested with bats. The report quoted the Bhopal scientists as saying that action had to be taken quickly to save the Taj from degradation.

Two months later the Times of India reported that its article had resulted in the appointment of 'a high-powered inter-ministerial committee' to look into the Taj's problems. It also said that the Prime Minister's office had called a meeting of experts who had decided that extensive investigations were necessary.

By this time the doors had been opened for some pretty trenchant newspaper satire. It was reported that an American couple had agreed to buy the Taj Mahal and take it home: 'One look and I wanted it so bad,' the wife gushed. A picture of the Taj in ruins, with one of its minarets fallen over to crack the dome like an egg (though they are designed to fall away) accompanied another lampooning effort. And there was a photograph of the Taj with its dome removed and oil refinery towers substituted.

The refinery was a particularly vexed issue and still attracts a good deal of criticism from conservationists who watch its statistics like hawks. Any change in the grade of crude oil processed, or production increases, leads to a spate of complaints. The refinery company, the government-owned Indian Oil Corporation, has responded with a public relations campaign describing the measures it has taken to prevent pollution.

Well before the refinery was commissioned, it says, a committee of experts from the Meteorological Department, the National Environmental Engineering Research Institute, the ASI, and the National Committee on Environmental Planning and Coordination was set up to examine problems which might arise. The refinery's pollution control systems, 'as practised in advanced countries,' include five air monitoring stations (including a mobile one) which began work before production began. These have permitted before and after studies which show no significant increase in pollution. Air around the refinery meets pollution control board standards and water is so well treated after use that farmers use it for irrigation.

More alarming were scientists' findings when they looked at the Taj Mahal's home town. The air of Agra itself turned out to be so polluted that the refinery at Mathura became a minor issue. More than two hundred iron foundries burning up to three thousand tonnes of coal a day were fouling the atmosphere, and so were two coal-burning power stations and coal-burning locomotives working in a railway yard just across the river from the Taj. There was pollution even from the burning ghats a few hundred yards upstream from the Taj where Agra's Hindus cremated their dead — at the rate of fifty or sixty bodies a day, with a tonne of firewood consumed for each one.

All this came to a head in the mid 1980s, and impressive action resulted. Though the foundries created more jobs than tourism did, a programme to move them to an industrial area north of the city got under way, along with campaigns to persuade owners to use cleaner coal and more efficient furnaces. The two power stations were closed down — no simple matter in a city with frequent electricity blackouts. Diesel engines replaced the coal-fired ones in the railway yard. Plans went ahead for an electric crematorium to be working by 1990, to put an end of those wood fires on the burning ghats.

And since the mood was right, moves began to shift a television tower which had been built east of the Taj, across the river, in a position where it too often showed up in long-lens photographs of the monument, usually between the right-hand minarets and the main building.

At the same time work began on a programme to plant fifty thousand trees a year, mainly by the Agra Development Authority. Agra's summer climate is so ferociously hot that many have died, despite watering by hand, but results can be seen in belts of vegetation along roadsides and along the Yamuna riverbank. (Another result is a proliferation of barbed wire fences to keep cattle, camels, goats and other animals from the struggling young trees. At first these fences appear ugly but you quickly learn to ignore them — their intention is what counts.) The trees planted, mostly spindly desert varieties, include nerium indica, which is said to absorb sulphur dioxide, a major pollutant.

In such ways has Agra's air pollution level been brought down from about a hundred micrograms of solid material to each cubic metre in 1977 to only eighteen in 1987. This compared, at that time, with sixty micrograms per cubic metre in Copenhagen, one hundred and ten in New York and two hundred and fifty in London.

Keeping bombs out of the Taj Mahal involves a different kind of scrutiny. It means security men at the main gate asking you to open your bag so they can look inside. It means uniformed men with guns sitting or strolling around. You may be able to work out from shoulder badges that some are from the Uttar Pradesh Home Guard, and you may not be much impressed by their ancient .303 rifles. Other men carry more formidable weapons. The security men you will not be aware of are those in plain clothes, always present and presumably just as interested in watching visitors to the Taj as I was, though for a different reason.

Along with the security watch go controls on camera tripods, because weapons could be disguised as tripods, and on photography in the tomb chambers, for a similar reason. The first of these controls is

Some security men you see. Some you do not . . .

accompanied by procedures whereby photographers can get permission from ASI headquarters in Delhi to use tripods, but the second is meant to be a total ban. A very senior ASI man told us that not even he could get photographs of the tombs. In practice, however, there is confusion.

Frequently there are no security men on duty in the tomb chambers, and even when there are it is difficult for them to prevent visitors taking out small cameras and snapping off a few shots. This can cause of good deal of resentment among tourists abiding by their guides' warnings that photography there is banned. Many of them feel that getting pictures or video tapes of the places they visit is what travel is all about.

The system needs to be sorted out, presumably in a manner to enforce the ban. Since security guards cannot be expected to recognise literally hundreds of different kinds of cameras brought in by tourists from all over the world — some of which look remarkably like grenades — a realistic policy would prevent any of them being taken into the building. Better this than that one day there is blood on the polished marble floor.

Meanwhile work being done to clean the air around the Taj Mahal is matched by work to clean the building itself. The ASI's researchers and consultants have found that a mixture of magnesium trisilicate and aluminium silicate can work wonders in removing accumulated grime and restoring the Makrana marble to its crystalline whiteness. We watched men at work and were surprised by the difference between cleaned and untreated areas. Some people who had known the Taj before disagreed but most Agrans, or Agrarians, we talked to thought the building looked cleaner than before.

Not only industrial deposits were being removed. A particular problem only recently solved was presented by the remains of a well-meant attempt at conservation in years past which had gone wrong. An acrylic resin coating which had been colourless when it was applied probably in the 1940s had yellowed with age. All concerned breathed easier when it was found that it could be removed without damaging the marble underneath.

A lesser difficulty is posed by the beehives which attach themselves to sheltered positions and quickly grow to big, black and ugly proportions. Iron-nerved men swing from rope ladders in the middle of the night, when the bees are drowsy, and deliver massive doses of insecticide. Early morning visitors to the Taj will find the hives gone and workers sweeping up thousands of dead insects.

Workers restore the Taj Mahal to whiteness.

Cleaning marble within the tomb chambers is technically not difficult — but if that marble is within reach of human hands it does not stay clean very long. Even the astonishing marble screen which surrounds the two tomb replicas, a world-class work of art, is stroked and caressed in a manner to astonish visitors used to the tight controls of European and American galleries and museums. Quickly it becomes discoloured with palm grease and perspiration, and the only answer, as mentioned earlier, may be to install railings to keep people away from it. Alternatively, in this hands-on age, perhaps hands on is the better way.

Another problem is more difficult. Any visitor strolling in the Taj gardens, and then north to where the building looks down on the Yamuna river, finds fascinating views over fields and villages. But the river itself is disappointing, especially in winter and summer. It is reputedly one of India's great waterways but one day I watched a dog cross from one side to the other without getting its belly wet. This in a river which old drawings show to be carrying sailing craft and where once the Mughals even moved armies by boat.

Worse, it stinks. Further upstream the Yamuna flows through Delhi, which takes virtually all its water for its city supply. Below Delhi the river comprises mainly whatever the city has returned to it through its drains and sewers. When even some of this is taken away

for irrigation, and when evaporation concentrates the rest, the result during the drier periods of the year is a noisome trickle. The smell may considerably disconcert our visitor as he looks out over those fields and villages.

Help may be at hand, though the manner in which I learned about it suggested yet another argument. The Times of India one day in February, 1988, printed an editorial titled, Goodbye Taj Mahal. The newspaper said it was appalled to read that the Indian government had asked the United States National Park Service to design a new layout for the gardens that surround the Taj. The rectangular Mughal

Old drawings show river traffic beside the Taj, but now the water is normally shallow. A development scheme could create a wide and attractive lake.

gardens were an integral part of the magnificent mausoleum, it continued, and there could be no explanation for the government's action except in terms of a blind obsession with American technology. The editorial warned that crass commercialism of the hamburger stands and amusement parks variety would destroy not only the Taj Mahal but also other monuments as well.

As so often happens, the editorial was based on wrong informa-

tion. American planners were going to be involved in a Taj project, but not in the Mughal gardens. The tourism ministry had been quietly acquiring land around the Taj, including a considerable tract across the Yamuna river, and the time had come to turn it all into a national park. The Americans had been asked to contribute ideas, and had agreed to do so. A National Parks Service spokesman said that sensitive development of the area would require the best talents of both countries working together 'to visualise the future of this outstanding World Heritage site'.

The national park area includes a tract of jungle — which in India means open scrub country — east of the Taj Mahal where deer and peafowl roam, an expanse of villages and farmland on the northern bank of the Yamuna, and a section of the Yamuna riverbed. It is not hard to envisage the creation of a lake beneath the Taj's tall walls

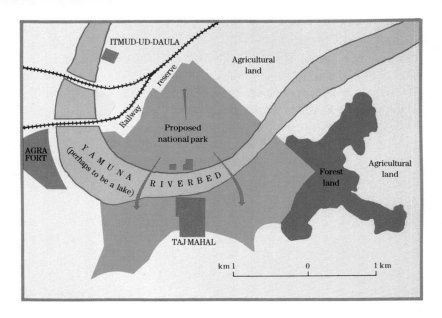

Nothing can exceed the fineness of the Taj Mahal; the excessive praise which generations of visitors have lavished upon it may excite our displeasure, but should not dull our perception of its magnificence; the perfect proportion of its parts, the justness of its setting, and the splendour of its material make it the highest point of Mughal building art — some would say of all building art — in India. —
A.A. Rizvi in Landmarks of South Asian Civilisation, New Delhi, 1983.

which would vastly improve its vistas — and which could even put an end to the stench. This would certainly be so if the scheme were matched by a broader one, similar to one to clean up the Ganges already under way, to reduce pollution throughout the length of the Yamuna.

Some ASI men are cautious about the proposal for a lake, pointing out that years ago they built earthworks in the riverbed to steer monsoon water away from the Taj Mahal's north wall. They are worried that an excess of water will damage the building's foundations. A lake would revive that danger, they say. But it is hard not to hope that answers can be found because the possibilities are spectacular.

'The ladies of the Mughal court had problems,' an Agra salesman declared. 'They had to share their husbands with all the other women in the harem. They had no power or rights of their own. They were prisoners. The only way they could assert themselves was by demanding the best in clothing, in jewellery, in whatever caught their fancy. They were like spoiled children.'

Their unworthy emotions, if we agree with that salesman, produced a worthy result. Their demands led to a hoard of dealers and artisans vying to display their wares in the markets that were attached to every court. And from that came an emphasis on quality in every aspect of creative endeavour.

Not much of it survived the fall of the empire, however. Excellence was not in such demand, especially when the British arrived with their emphasis on railways and factories and law courts instead of the other kind. In one corner of Agra, however, an unsung part of the old tradition plodded on, and a few years ago it burst into bloom.

The tradition was silk embroidery, perhaps with gold and silver threads as well. It was kept alive by some diligent practitioners, and in the 1950s one of them tried something new. Sheikh Shams Uddin had mastered the craft from his father, and then he made it three-dimensional, using stitch upon stitch. It was a move that made him famous, with awards flowing in and his work displayed all over the world.

Shortly before this book was written, two of his huge

embroideries were displayed at a
Festival of India in the United
States. Surprisingly for a Muslim
artist working in a mainly Hindu
country, they depicted Jesus and
Moses. At the same time examples
of his earlier work, including a
grand depiction of the peacock
throne, were on permanent display in an Agra jewellery shop.
The doorway of Sheikh Shams
Uddin's house in the crowded
centre of old Agra carries a
plaque, the result of an award
from Delhi, which names him a
'master craftsman of India'.

'All these honours have come to
me from God's grace,' he said
when we called. 'My ancestors laid
down the tradition so that from
childhood I was able to
concentrate on it. It is God's grace
that I was able to do something
new.' Even so, it was a sad
interview as this honoured old
man, small and white-haired, was

almost blind. At the age of 72, he
had lost the use of one eye and had
a cataract in the other. He had
undergone operations in the United States and India, and no one
knew if he would see again.

His three sons, carrying on in
their father's name, take visitors
around their workshop where
craftsmen produce work to their
father's specifications. 'But they
will never be as good as he was,'
one of the sons said. 'He was an
artist as well as a craftsman. He
had tremendous talent and
tremendous patience. He was
ruthless about discarding pieces
he thought not up to standard —
even after weeks of work. His work
is incredible. Now he has given
his eyes for his art.'

People who know Sheikh Shams
Uddin and his work well are not
optimistic that his standards will
be maintained. 'Today's students
don't have the same talent, the
same sense of colour or fineness
or design, or anything. Their
work is just a poor copy of the
master's,' said a jeweller who sells
Sheikh Shams Uddin's work.

'Good artisans are hard to
find,' another of his sons said.
'They need about five years' train-
ing. But they come here only long
enough to get the idea, and then
they open their own shops.' Why
not employ women? 'They don't
have the patience.' But the real
reason for not using women, as
with marble work, is that they

The photograph of Sheikh Shams Uddin is published by courtesy of his sons.

*'marry out' and would take their
skills with them.*

*Mughal courts were great
consumers of carpets, mainly
from Persia, for decoration, to
soften the floors of their stone
palaces and bring a touch of
warmth during winter. But
manufacturing in India (except
in Kashmir) never really caught
on. Even today carpets made in
Agra are not highly regarded.
Attempts are being made to
change this, however, with
Kashmiri specialists inviting
boys to join in a manufacturing*

*operation. Some good results come
from their labours but the work is
hard and slow: a carpet less than
two metres long can take six
months' work. So recruitment is
difficult. 'No one really wants to
be a weaver,' one of the teachers
commented. 'Boys would sooner
be rickshaw drivers or join the
army.'*

The small silk carpet above is also from Sheikh Shams Uddin's workshop. It is 18 inches x 24 inches.

Mumtaz Mahal

The woman whom the Taj Mahal has made immortal was born in 1594 and named Arjumand Banu (which is rendered in various spellings). She was a well favoured child, daughter of Asaf Khan, who would become one of the most powerful men in the court of the Mughal Emperor Jahangir; and niece of the woman who would become Jahangir's wife. Jahangir was a son of the Emperor Akbar, one of the ablest leaders the world has ever seen, the man who turned the Mughal's tenuous hold on northern India into a great empire. Akbar ruled through the first nine years of Arjumand's life.

Akbar's career can be compared with that of the first Queen Elizabeth of England, and there is a startling parallel between their reigns. They came to power within three years of each other, ruled for more than fifty years, and died within three years of each other. Arjumand Banu would certainly have heard of that other empire, and may even have seen, through the palace grills which permitted women of the court to see without being seen, European ambassadors as they arrived to present their credentials. There was not much that went on in the Mughal palaces that the women did not know about. More, once her aunt Mehr-un-Nissa, later Nur Jahan, had

This engaging, birdseye view of court life in Mughal India is from Francois Valentyn's Old and New India, published in 1726. Colour was added later.

married Jahangir, there was even less that Arjumand did not learn. Nur Jahan was a formidable woman, according to writer Kanwar Lal 'one of the most beautiful, cultured, elegant, gracious, gifted, taste-endowed and talent-possessing queens in the world's history'. This seems fair, and in a fairer world she would be better known today, certainly more famous than her immortal niece. But while Nur Jahan was headed for power, Arjumand was destined for a kind of romance.

Also in the court was Prince Khurram, Jahangir's son by another wife, born in 1592. According to Muni Lal, who has written a superb series of books about the Mughal emperors, Khurram grew up to be a strong-limbed boy of considerable intelligence and down to earth commonsense. He was such a likely lad, indeed, that his two older brothers, Khusrau and Parvez, were disgruntled by the favours showered on him. That the Emperor Akbar doted on his precocious grandson did not help matters.

In 1605 Akbar died. Jahangir (previously known as Prince Salim) succeeded him and and promptly embarked on a life of what Muni Lal describes as 'sensual levities'. He became particularly addicted to drinking, at times lacing his wine with opium for greater effect. This irked Prince Khusrau, a quiet young man, so much that he listened too well when courtiers persuaded him that he should be emperor. In 1606 he revolted against his father, only to be quickly captured, part-ially blinded as punishment and locked in prison.

His followers were more hideously dealt with, most dying under torture. Many were impaled and while they yet lived Khusrau, still sighted, was invited to accept their agonised writhings as the salutes of faithful retainers. The glitter of the court had a pitch black side as well.

Khurram was close enough to these events to study and learn from them. When the time came he would prove even more ruthless than his father — and before then would also revolt. In the meantime he stood first in Jahangir's favour, and doubtless thought it only proper that his father should select one of the court's most beautiful young women as his first wife. Khurram's engagement to Arjumand Banu was announced in March, 1607. He was fifteen, she thirteen,

There is no doubt that Arjumand was comely, even at that age, though later a courtly writer was perhaps merely doing his job when he recorded that she was so beautiful 'that the moon hid its face in shame'. Paintings in the Mughal style which show her to have been a real stunner seem to be comparatively recent creations, done per-haps to meet the demand which grew up as the story of the Taj Mahal began to spread around the world. They could be entirely works of imagination or they could be copies of works which indeed depicted Arjumand but which have since been lost.

There is considerable doubt whether Khurram had any say in the matter of his engagement; Arjumand certainly would not have done. There is no evidence at all to support the popular story that Khurram and Arjumand had earlier known and admired each other after meeting at a court bazaar wherein women were able to unveil themselves and offer items for sale. The story has it that Arjumand displayed her wares, her beauty and her wit all at the same time when Khurram came to her stall, and that romance bloomed. It is an engaging story, but nothing more.

Let us assume however that the two teenagers were smitten with each other. Jahangir was also smitten with love, for Mehr-un-Nissa, later Nur Jahan, the daughter of Ghyas Beg, who would become his prime minister — and the wife of one of his most powerful provincial governors. It was clear the husband had to die, and he did, by most accounts violently.

Those critics who have objected to the effeminacy of the architecture [of the Taj Mahal] unconsciously pay the highest tribute to the genius of the builders. The whole conception, and every line and detail of it, express the intention of the designers. It is Mumtaz Mahal herself, radiant in her youthful beauty, who still lingers on the banks of the shining Yamuna. — E.B. Havell, author of various works on Indian art and architecture around the turn of this century.

But Jahangir was unable to work his will with Mehr-un-Nissa, who may have had some reservations about a suitor with blood on his hands. Her position was weak, however, and eventually she began to respond to Jahangir's advances, demanding marriage or nothing. It makes sense to see the engagement between Khurram and Arjumand, Mehr's niece, as nothing more than a move in Jahangir's chess game to win his heart's desire.

If this were so, this path of true love could not be smooth. First there came a distraction. Jahangir decided on an expedition to Kabul, in today's Afghanistan. Khurram was made leader of the royal entourage. Half-blind Khusrau could still foment trouble and was too dangerous to be left behind, so he travelled in chains like a criminal. In Kabul, perhaps feeling he had nothing more to lose, Khusrau joined in another conspiracy. Khurram learned of it, trapped the plotters, earned praise, and put an end to any ambitions Khusrau may have retained. (Years later, in 1622, he would as ruthlessly end Khusrau's life, having him murdered lest he complicate Khurram's road to the throne.)

On his return from Kabul, Jahangir pressed Mehr, by this time widowed, to marry him. She stalled. Jahangir used every trick he could think of to make her change her mind, threatening at one stage to call off the engagement between Khurram and Arjumand and to strip Mehr's family of honours and property. In the end, after three years, Mehr gave in — as she always had intended to, once she had Jahangir totally besotted, hers to hold for ever.

Her method worked and her marriage to Jahangir in 1611 was successful. In the process, however, Khurram and Arjumand found delay giving way to disaster. As part of his political footwork, Jahangir announced Khurram's betrothal to a descendant of Shah Ismail of Persia, and they were married in October, 1610. There was one child, a daughter, before she was laden with gifts and sent back home. At the time of the marriage a stricken Arjumand set about assuaging her grief by learning the Koran by heart. The remedy worked. As Muni Lal tells it, 'she developed in her a spiritual glow which gave her shapely form a poise as dignified as it was relaxed'. She began to feel that all eventually would be well.

Once Jahangir had married Mehr, who was given the title Nur Jahan, or Light of the World, the way was clear for Khurram and Arjumand to marry, and they did, on 28 April, 1612. He was twenty, she eighteen. She was given the title, Mumtaz Mahal, or Chosen One of the Palace. The first of their children, a daughter, was born the following year but lived only three years. Their second, another girl,

We do not know what Mumtaz Mahal looked like but portraits of Nur Jahan, her illustrious aunt, do exist. This brilliant work, titled Jahangir embracing Nur Jahan, is a splendid specimen of Mughal art. It is dated around 1615. Since Mumtaz Mahal and Shah Jahan had been married three years at that time, it is easy to imagine them in a similar situation — with the exception that Shah Jahan was well built and had aquiline features. Jahangir was a patron of art, as Shah Jahan was of architecture, and it is likely he would have known of and approved this painting. The presence of serving women is illustrative of harem life in the Mughal court, for they were always on hand to help if needed, and even to take part in the most intimate occasions. The painting is done in ink, colour and gold on paper, and is 33.3cm x 20.9cm. It is reproduced by permission of the Los Angeles County Museum of Art, from the Nasli & Alice Heeramaneck Collection, Museum Acquisition Fund.

Jahanara, was born in March, 1614, and twelve more followed in the next fifteen years. Only seven of the fourteen (born in 1614, 1615, 1616, 1617, 1618, 1624 and 1631) survived to adulthood. There were also some miscarriages. Arjumand died giving birth to their last child when she was thirtyeight or thirtynine.

Among Arjumand's wedding presents was a gold plaque from Nur Jahan, inscribed with a couplet which passed on a message which Nur Jahan had received on her wedding day, from her mother. Obey your husband always with a smile, she was told. In her message to Arjumand, she said that loyalty and obedience were the finest treasures a woman could offer a man. When she died nineteen years later, that gold plaque was found in a casket near her bed. Shah Jahan treasured it for the rest of his life as a reminder of her devotion.

Soon after their wedding Khurram was attending to imperial matters as well. When risings against Mughal rule away to the south became intolerable, he was given an army and sent to solve the problem. He waged total war, not just against the enemy but against the entire population of the region. Here is Muni Lal again: 'Villages were razed, standing crops set on fire, all exits were sealed, wells and tanks poisoned, the [enemy] army was chased relentlessly from one hideout to another, blockades of towns and cities tightened to the point where not an ant could crawl through, barbaric punishments were given to those found collaborating with [the enemy], bridges were wrecked and roads and tracks planted with death-scattering dynamite.'

The enemy surrendered and Khurram was so magnanimous that there was no more trouble for nearly fifty years. Khurram returned home a hero and in 1617 was given the title Shah Jahan, or Ruler of the World. There seemed to be no doubt that he would one day succeed Jahangir as emperor. He gained in stature. He and Mumtaz, as Muni Lal puts it, 'made a complete whole'. She provided 'soul-strength for her husband's surging ambition and his limitless lust for power'.

So limitless, indeed, that after more victories Nur Jahan, by this time virtual ruler of the empire as her husband ruined his health with debauchery, became worried. She came to feel that Khurram, now Shah Jahan, might not wait for Jahangir's death to claim his throne. She began to feel that a son-in-law, Shahryar (husband of her daughter by her first marriage), might be a better bet as successor; certainly he would be more tractable, a figurehead through whom Nur Jahan could continue to wield power.

The politics which followed, the orders and deceptions, the marches and counter-marches, the confusions and treacheries, are too complicated to be gone into here. But they led to Shah Jahan, who had been campaigning once more in the south, marching on Agra while his father was away in Kashmir. His army looted the city but a gallant commander kept the Fort, the seat of power, safe for Jahangir and Nur Jahan.

Now there was no pretence. Shah Jahan was in revolt against his father. Jahangir ordered his top general, Mahabat Khan, 'to rub his son's nose in the dust of humiliation'. A great battle near Delhi resulted. Shah Jahan was defeated and fled back south. He had left Mumtaz there with the other women of his court and doubtless looked to her — by this time inevitably pregnant once more — for solace. It was a role she would play frequently in the years to come as Jahangir hounded Shah Jahan across India.

A building wastefully without a function; it is only a despot's monument to a woman, not of India, who bore a child every year for fifteen years. — V.S. Naipaul, in An Area of Darkness, London, 1964.

(One recent account of her life says that during battles she stayed by her husband's side, ready to wipe away the dust, blood and weariness of battle and to pour wine for his parched lips and thirsty throat. In fact the Mughals took good care that their women were kept far from the fighting. 'He that has wives and mistresses on the battlefield has given hostages to fortune,' said Babar, founder of the dynasty. He never in his life wore armour in the presence of women. Humayun broke this rule and suffered for it. Akbar loved women but left them at home when he went campaigning. Jahangir was never involved in battle anyway, preferring to be with women. Shah Jahan always made sure that his women were locked up securely and well guarded before he rode into action.)

Shah Jahan marched his army south. Nur Jahan contrived to have his brother, Prince Parvez, placed at the head of the pursuing Mughal army, though it was clear that Mahabat Khan would make the important decisions. The pressure on Shah Jahan's men was so great that a mutiny broke out, and order was restored only after two thousand men had been executed.

Shah Jahan wrote to Parvez seeking a settlement but negotiations led to a betrayal so shocking that it is said that Shah Jahan's hair turned white overnight — just as it was said that his hair turned white after the death of his wife eight years later. His position seemed hopeless and he faced the prospect of being dragged home in chains and then perhaps murdered.

In the evening I walked about the noble terrace and luxuriant gardens [and] also rambled about every part of the Taje itself, enjoying a feast that seemed too great for me alone. . . . Nothing in architecture can well exceed the beauty of this structure viewed from my pavilion at the corner of the grand terrace. — Thomas Twining, who was living in the Taj grounds, 1790s.

Desperate times demand desperate solutions. Shah Jahan took his army east, right across India, to Orissa. The province, unaware of danger, fell into his hands, and so did Bengal. It seemed Shah Jahan's star was rising again. He seized Bihar. And he prepared to march once more on Agra. His scheme looked feasible but it reckoned without Nur Jahan and Mahabat Khan. Though possessed of little reliable information, they were able once more to confront Shah Jahan with a massive army.

Defeat was inevitable. A day of ferocious fighting ended with Shah Jahan, wounded in the shoulder, fleeing 'through a corridor of dead bodies'. He stopped at a village to eat and have his wound bandaged, then headed for the great fort of Rohtas in Bihar — where Mumtaz was about to give birth to a son, Murad. This should have been a happy augury, but in fact bad was to grow much worse. Within days he was fleeing once more, leaving Mumtaz in the safety of Rohtas.

He recrossed India — only to be confronted once more by Parvez and Mahabat Khan. All looked black until Parvez offered a deal. This was not entirely out of benevolence. Parvez, first in line for the throne, wanted to get back to the capital, where Nur Jahan was promoting Shahryar's case. Shah Jahan, desperate, accepted harsh conditions, including his remaining in the south, in return for an end to the war. He had been given time to plot again.

Intrigue back in the capital came to his rescue. Not everyone at court looked forward to having Shahryar, a colourless man, on the throne with Nur Jahan using him like a puppet. Parvez had a following, until he died of pleasurable indulgences. Nur Jahan feared that Mahabat was too powerful and ordered him to Bengal. But he did not go; instead he staged a coup, holding Jahangir and Nur Jahan briefly prisoner. When that was settled, the three sons of Jahangir's younger brother Daniyal appeared as contenders for parts of the apparently crumbling empire (and eventually would die for their presumption). All was confusion.

Then Jahangir died, in October, 1927. Shahryar in Lahore proclaimed himself emperor but Nur Jahan's brother Asaf Khan (Mumtaz's father) would have none of it. He and others opposed to Nur Jahan's scheming put Khusrau's son Dawar Baksh on the throne as a stop-gap, sent an army to put down Shahryar (who was blinded and jailed), and set in train events which would see Nur Jahan a virtual prisoner for the rest of her life, devoted to religion. Asaf Khan also sent a message to Shah Jahan. The throne awaits you, it said.

There was much to be done. A father to be mourned, plotters to be forestalled, enemies to be accounted for, other claimants (including

Dawar Baksh) ruthlessly to be disposed of, delegations to be entertained, a long journey of pomp and circumstance back to Agra to be undertaken. Shah Jahan's escort on that journey was provided by Mahabat Khan, the man who had bedevilled and frustrated his life as a rebel. Their vast procession reached the outskirts of Agra in January, 1628, and in February, after a twelve-day wait while astronomers squabbled over auspicious days, entered the city. It had been a long and troubled wait, but now he was emperor.

And Mumaz was first lady of the land. She had borne Shah Jahan four surviving sons and two surviving daughters, who all were to share with her in the distribution of honours that attended Shah Jahan's investiture. The years of turmoil and anxiety as they fled continually from imperial armies were behind them. There was only happiness to look forward to.

A thorn in Shah Jahan's side during his early military campaigns and again during his revolt against his father was a Portuguese settlement on the Hugli river, near modern Calcutta. It had existed since Humayun's time, and had grown large, rich and intolerant. Twice (once as an imperial soldier, once as a rebel) Shah Jahan had asked the Portuguese for help and twice he had been rebuffed. The Encyclopaedia Britannica says that the Portuguese considered that no faith needed to be kept with an infidel, and that to this policy of perfidy they added a tendency to cruelty beyond the normal limits of a very rough age. As a result they lost any Indian sympathy they might have got.

With relations already bad, the Portuguese made them worse by abducting two of Mumtaz's slave girls, whose fate remained unknown. Shah Jahan chose to see this affront as a mortal one. When he became emperor the Portuguese in Hugli knew they were in for trouble. Mahabat Khan was given the job of taking Hugli from the insolent Europeans, and organised a force of six thousand horsemen, fifteen thousand foot soldiers, one hundred war elephants and seven hundred armed boats. Then came another abduction, of a high-born Mughal woman with her daughter and daughter-in-law, who also were never heard of again. This fuelled Mughal anger and added to a lengthening list of complaints against the Portuguese.

The first Mughal attack was repulsed with heavy losses but the Portuguese knew they were vulnerable and tried vainly to negotiate. The Mughals were determined to wipe their settlement from the map and eventually did so, though they lost nearly ten thousand men in the process to Portuguese guns. The Portuguese top brass managed to escape by ship at the last moment but hundreds more were left behind, captured and marched off to Agra, a trek so long and hard that many died on the way.

Never before had Agra seen so many white men and women. Shah Jahan ordered those men who chose to become Muslims to be set free and given employment; the rest were imprisoned, though most were later released and enabled to reach another Portuguese settlement at Goa. The women went to harems, either as members or as servants. The price of failure in those days was harsh indeed.

The point about this, in a chapter about Mumtaz Mahal, is that she has been charged with a role in the persecution of the Portuguese captives. She may indeed have influenced Shah Jahan in his animosity towards the Hugli settlement, as she was much involved when it refused help; and she was certainly involved when her serving women were kidnapped. But she was dead before that pathetic column of prisoners crept into Agra, and to the fates that awaited them there.

Attempts to determine her character, in this and other matters, are bedevilled by lack of evidence. Court reports are not greatly to be relied on, as their writers knew what was expected of them, and other reports are scanty. One writer, K.C. Mazumdar, says that Mumtaz inspired Shah Jahan to acts of charity and benevolence and filled his heart with mercy for the weak and needy. She is reported to have organised charities and helped unmarried young women find husbands. But we shall never know if anything she did in this line exceeded the duties that went with her position — just as we shall never know whether she was really as cruel as some other writers say. Did she really enjoy watching prisoners, especially Christian missionaries, being tortured? It was a cruel and bloodthirsty age, and perhaps women of the palace did so divert themselves.

The main reason we shall never know much about Mumtaz Mahal is that the time during which she might have made a name for herself, in one way or another, was drastically cut short. Less than four years after that grand entry into Agra and her husband's enthronement, she was dead.

It has been said that the Deccan, the south of India, is the graveyard of the Mughal empire. Emperor after emperor felt he had to keep it suppressed, and time after time armies were sent off to achieve generally half-hearted victories. The south was a sink which endlessly consumed Mughal men and money. The south was Shah Jahan's destination once more, soon after he became emperor, at the head of yet another army.

Invitations (which would have amounted to orders) were issued to twentyone leading women in the harem to join the expedition. Mumtaz Mahal, though three months' pregnant with her fourteenth child, was one of them. Special arrangements were made for her comfort. Dancers, musicians, artists and men of learning also went along. The long journey began by boat, Shah Jahan and his staff in one, the women, well guarded and screened, in another. The huge force of horsemen, elephants, foot soldiers and camp followers trudged overland. Weeks of marching brought Shah Jahan and his army to Burhanpur, where a vast camp was built.

Or perhaps camp is the wrong word. An English traveller who saw such a Mughal base described it as 'admirably arranged and occupying a circumference of at least twenty miles'. He continued: 'Looking down on it from a height, it resembled a beautiful city of many coloured tents; that of the emperor in the centre, with its gilded globes and pinnacles forming a sort of castle, from whence diverged numerous streets, laid out without the least disorder, since everyone, whether noble or shopkeeper, knew the precise spot on which he must place himself by its distance from, and situation with regard to, the royal pavilion.'

A camp such as this was Shah Jahan's base for battle. All war is grotesque, but this campaign which he waged in the south was horrifying even by the standards of those bloody times. It was so obscene as to arouse even in Shah Jahan doubts about the use of victories attained at such cost. He paused to consider whether or not to march on to further battles. And then he received news that Mumtaz Mahal had given birth to their child, but was very ill. He was with her when she died early the next morning (probably on 7 June, 1631). The emperor was laid low by the news, lower than by any possible defeat at the hands of the enemy.

Building the Monument

There is a story, based on pretty skimpy evidence, that Mumtaz Mahal, as she lay dying, asked Shah Jahan to build a splendid mausoleum over her grave. Or perhaps it was his own idea. One of the startling details about this famous building is how little is known about its origins. In the absence of facts, stories have sprung up to fill the gaps.

One says that when Shah Jahan had decided on his vastly expensive project, he summoned possible architects to the bank of the Yamuna river, and there placed each one beside a mound of gold coins. 'Shovel them into the river,' he commanded. Most were so awed by the wealth in front of them that they were unable to obey, or if they did they lacked enthusiasm. Only one fell eagerly to his task — and he, of course, was given the job of building the Taj Mahal. Shah Jahan wanted a man who would not bother to count the cost; what mattered was getting the job done.

Another story is that his architect, no matter how chosen, came to display a certain lack of understanding of what was expected of him. 'He has not experienced real sorrow, so he does not know what I want,' Shah Jahan decided. So he had the architect's wife beheaded to help him see the light.

As for the fate of architects and artisans alike once they had fin-

The Taj Mahal combines size and simplicity with fine detail, so there is always something more to perceive.

ished their work, there are numerous stories that they were either killed, blinded or had their hands chopped off so they would never again be able to create such beauty. There is nothing to support any of these stories.

The fact is that facts are few. Not even the idea that the dying Mumtaz made last requests of her husband is borne out by contemporary records. Of course she would get her monument, since the Mughals, being Muslims, buried their dead, usually with an appropriate building above. Not for them the cremations of the Hindus whom they ruled. It is also said that Mumtaz asked her husband not to marry again, which could well have stemmed (if it happened) from her concern that their sons would not be joined by more eventual contenders for the throne.

Just what happened that night will never be known, but one writer has managed at least to make it an extraordinarily long night. It was after midnight, he wrote, when Shah Jahan learned that his wife, who had just given birth to a daughter, wished to rest. He also retired, only to be awakened 'a few hours later' to be told that Mumtaz had had a relapse and was asking for him. He went to her at once, and spent 'several hours' talking by her bedside until she lost consciousness 'in the early hours of the morning' and died.

What is certain is that Shah Jahan was so shocked by the loss of his wife that he ceased to function effectively as emperor. He arranged for Mumtaz's body to be sent back to Agra, with their second son Muhammad Shuja in charge of the cortege and Mumtaz's favourite companion, Sati-un-Nisa Khanam, also in attendance. This was a role she would continue to play even after death, being buried just outside the wall of the Taj Mahal. The sorrowful procession took three months to reach Agra.

Meanwhile Shah Jahan, his hair it is said turned white (again), tried to continue his military campaign, but his heart was not in it. The following March he set out for home again, his army moving slowly northwards through the waxing heat of summer which would have curtailed such diversions as hunting and musical evenings even if the emperor had still been interested in them. He was not, and the eventual arrival in Agra was totally unlike the ceremonial departure the previous year. A saddened emperor, grieving his lost wife and worried that his military campaign had been a failure, made all around him melancholy as well.

This mood could well have persisted, inevitably at great cost to the empire, had not a man named Mulla Farid, astronomer, savant and old friend, come to Shah Jahan. According to Muni Lal, he spoke to Shah Jahan in these terms: 'Death is not the end, only a new beginning. Love never perishes; it is a fire which cannot be extinguished even by the worst storms of fate. The most revered queen is no longer by your side, Sire, but believe me, O Monarch of Monarchs, that she will remain with you for as long as the earth keeps revolving on its axis. The spirit, like love, is indestructible. Not even the waters of a thousand rivers will be able to quench the light that she lit. . . . [She] is alive not only in her love and goodness but also in the four sturdy sun-like sons she blessed you with. Shed your anguish and let your subjects bask once again in the sunshine of your good cheer.'

The advice worked. In Muni Lal's words, 'Shah Jahan's grief first turned into the neutral grey of tranquillity and then burgeoned into the blazing red of joyous living which gave his reign a splendour of its own'. Other commentators agree that he brought the Mughal dynasty in north India to heights of brilliance it had never seen before and would never see again. For all his faults, Shah Jahan was the grandest of the six men who would be called emperor before irreversible decline set in. That the later part of his career would submerge him in pathos and tragedy does nothing to alter this.

It was the Ivory Gate through which all good dreams come; it was the realisation of the gleaming halls of dawn that Tennyson sings of. . . . and over and above concrete comparisons, it seemed the embodiment of all things pure, all things holy, and all things unhappy. — Rudyard Kipling.

His first task was to order the construction of Mumtaz Mahal's mausoleum, which would be as grand as genius and money could make it. There is no doubt that in this he was moved by memories of their love, though at least one Indian writer, P.N. Oak, has complained that this is to 'argue backwards' — to believe that because Shah Jahan spent so much on the Taj he must have loved Mumtaz. This is extreme, but it may be allowed that Shah Jahan felt himself impelled also by the political need to make his mark on a capital not accustomed to his ways. Since becoming emperor only five years before he had been away for more than a year, and word of his indecisive military campaign in the south was doing him no good. Wearing a crown is an uneasy business.

Once word went out that Shah Jahan planned a mausoleum, there would have been no dearth of ideas and talent arriving in his court from even the distant parts of his empire, and perhaps beyond. It must be presumed that the emperor set up a kind of committee to examine all ideas, and to send the best of them on to another committee which he himself would head. Their tasks would have been to find an architect, and a design.

For some years the man given credit as architect of the Taj Mahal was Ustad Isa. But who was he? Ustad simply means a teacher or master craftsman of some sort and Isa is a common Muslim name. More, his name was variously rendered and he was reported to have come from all manner of places. David Carroll, in his book on the Taj Mahal, said moreover that Ustad Isa's name did not appear until the beginning of the nineteenth century, when it found its way into every travel guide. He concluded that Ustad Isa 'is probably a fictitious amalgam of Muslim-sounding names, most likely the invention of latter-day British guidebook writers'.

Not so much a building as an exercise in pure mathematics. —
Source unknown.

More recently a man named Ustad Ahmad Lahori (Master Ahmad from Lahore) has been more reliably identified as the Taj Mahal's chief architect, in the practice of those days not so much the designer as the man who pulled the strings together. An inscription on his grave in Aurangabad says he built the Taj Mahal and the Jame Mosque in Delhi, and there is other evidence as well.

Quickly — because the site had been chosen and levelling and foundation work had begun — a likely design was selected and a panel of experts set up to find ways to make it perfect. It had to be perfect because Shah Jahan would brook nothing less, and because the Islamic building code forbade changes once construction had begun.

An Indian novelist writing in English, T.N. Murari, has written a fascinating account, based on much study, of what he thinks happened. In his book Taj (London, 1985), he describes a gathering of architects, builders, calligraphers, lapidaries of great skill, all confronted with a wooden model, 'the silent ghost that haunted their lives'. It was familiar, with the form of monuments they knew, but strange also with cleaner and sharper lines. It had come to Shah Jahan in dreams but it was incomplete. The great men had made countless suggestions but the furious emperor had rejected them all.

Meanwhile, in workshops attached to the palace, hundreds of men bent over their drawings, designing the most intricate patterns and shapes for the interior walls. Murari writes that the emperor drove them hard, 'rejecting most of the work, wanting it refined still further, made yet more beautiful until all the original ideas and designs had been lost a dozen times over. They were to imitate everything yet nothing. It was as if in the purity of wrought flowers Shah Jahan wished to purge the opulence of his power. . . . He was trying to balance the suffocating and ornate magnificence of the Great Mughal with the simplicity of his obsessive love for his queen.'

Later Shah Jahan felt the dome had not achieved perfection. A designer told him a dome could be but one shape, and was rewarded with a glance like a sword-slash. Murari continues: "This dome will be different," Shah Jahan said. "It will be round, drawn up, as if it would float away."

'The emperor's hand hovered in the air as if he held an invisible ball. . . . His glance fell on the slave girls and he beckoned one; she knelt by him. He exposed her breast; it was small and firm with a dark nipple. He clutched it but it did not satisfy him, so he beckoned another girl. Her breasts were larger, high, round and firm. The chill teased her nipples. He held one breast, squeezing and reshaping it.

"'Like this, like this, you see.'"

The architect was told to measure the proportions of the breast, which he did with calipers while the girl remained passive, staring into the distance.

I wrote to Mr Murari, asking if he had found anything in his reading to support this version. He replied that the passage involved literary licence but was based on something factual. 'The Taj is the most feminine of Mughal buildings and I wanted somehow to express this femininity,' he said.

A cogent and pleasing point about Murari's treatment of the story is that it places Shah Jahan fairly in centre stage as the man who made the important decisions. There is never just one designer of any complicated building. A famous name may get the credit but in fact the owner of that name would have drawn both on history and on current ideas and suggestions from many sources. Shah Jahan did just that. He determined what the building would look like, and that in modern terms makes him the architect. After more than three hundred years this perhaps does not matter much, but Shah Jahan has been so maligned in other ways that he should get credit for this.

This would also settle claims that the architect was a European. There were itinerant Europeans in and around the Mughal court while the Taj Mahal was being built, mostly soldiers of fortune engaged to handle new-fangled cannonry but with some men of talent and culture among them. Yet it passes belief that any one of them could have so absorbed the architecture of the region and become so established that his ideas would be accepted. Indeed, as infidels they would not have been trusted in any responsible role.

Some European writers went to great lengths in their efforts to show that such and such an Italian or Frenchman was the key man, and some of their claims were long accepted. But not today. Much excellent research work has gone into analysing the records, and most opinion today is that there is no more substance to these old stories than there is to the myth that Shah Jahan planned a black marble replica of the Taj on the opposite bank of the Yamuna river.

When Mumtaz Mahal's body arrived in Agra, it was laid in a temporary grave in the garden of a riverside mansion belonging to a Rajput noble, Raja Jai Singh of Amber, a grandson of one of Akbar's

*H*ow to design a Taj Mahal

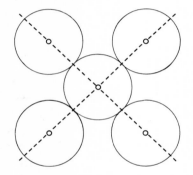 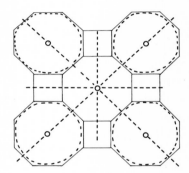

most capable generals. This suggests that Shah Jahan, though still away in the south, had already decided that this would be the site of her mausoleum; otherwise her temporary grave would probably have been in the Fort. Raja Jai Singh is said to have offered to give up the land without payment but custom demanded that he be compensated, and he was given three other houses.

At least, this is almost certainly what happened but writer P.N. Oak, mentioned earlier, does not agree. In a book titled The Taj Mahal is a Hindu Palace (Bombay, 1969), he protests that the standard version, along with all books except his own published during the past three hundred years, are based on pure fantasy. He expresses his wonder that people the world over believe 'the arrant nonsense that a stupendous and fabulous monument like the Taj Mahal could at all be raised, at least in India, to commemorate carnal love'. 'Such puerile credulity may be all right in the mumbo-jumbo of romantic fiction,' he says, 'but it is hardly justified in the context of the hard facts of Muslim courts in mediaeval India.'

Oak's thesis is that the Taj Mahal was originally a Hindu palace, and that all Shah Jahan did was confiscate it, toss out its owner and give it a marble coating. 'Camouflaging Hindu buildings with Muslim lettering was not Shah Jahan's innovation,' he says. 'It has a hoary tradition.' Both Humayun's tomb in Delhi and Akbar's on the outskirts of Agra were originally Hindu palaces, he continues.

More, the Taj Mahal does not derive its name from Mumtaz Mahal; rather it is the other way around — she derived her title after death

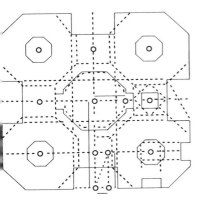

Scholars have worked out that the design of the Taj Mahal could have started with the circle in the centre of the first of these drawings. Four more circles of the same size spaced around it would have provided the basic shape. The next step would be to turn the circles into octagons, as in the second drawing, with connecting walls added as well. From this it would be a fairly simple matter to arrive at the final shape shown in the third drawing. The shape is both elegant and structurally suited to the huge weight of the dome which would go on top.

from the name of her tomb, which was originally Taja Maha Alaya, Sanskrit for 'resplendent shrine'. The building originated in the 12th Century as a temple for Shiva, Oak maintains. The villain behind this deception, he charges, is Shah Jahan, a man he describes as 'proud, presumptuous, haughty, over-bearing, stingy, hard-headed and hard-hearted', and also conceited, bigotted, fanatical, cruel and lecherous.

However, there is a certain stridency to Oak's writing which makes it less than convincing. Were his book more coolly written, the archaeologists and historians who must answer Oak's assault on conventional teaching would have to work harder. As it is, they generally have little trouble finding evidence, often technical — as in the composition of the Taj Mahal's mortar — to rebut his ideas. No responsible historian takes Oak's claims seriously, I was told on several occasions.

It appears then that the site chosen for the Taj Mahal, almost due east of the Fort and about the size of three football fields, had to be cleared before work could begin. Even before the design of the mausoleum was decided on, thousands of people were put to work preparing foundations and diverting the Yamuna river to create a lake next to the site — just such a lake as may be rebuilt in the closing years of the Twentieth Century.

The foundations are complicated. According to M.C. Joshi (now joint director-general of the ASI) in a paper published in 1973, the deepest parts of the Taj consist of a series of deep 'wells' packed with rubble bound together with lime inside, and surrounded by stone masonry — a common Mughal practice. Piers were built at close intervals on these wells, with a series of arches above to support a compact bed of masonry. The main building stands on this bed. Joshi comments that all possible precautions were taken to protect the foundations against the thrust of water from the Yamuna river.

Other reports say that bricks used in the foundations above the normal waterline were soaked in hot fat to make them impervious for centuries to come, and the masonry was bound together with that same mortar which the Archaeological Survey of India still uses today. The builders knew what they were doing; in more than three hundred years, despite alternating floods and droughts, there has been no subsidence. Nor has any flood climbed high enough to enter the main building.

(There is a story about the foundations too, which says that their builder completed his work — and then vanished for a year. During this time it was feared that he had run away because something was wrong, so work on the mausoleum was suspended. Then one day the builder happily presented himself to Shah Jahan, announced that his foundations had passed the tests he had posed for them, and that work could go ahead. Shah Jahan asked why he had disappeared. It was the only way to make you stop work, the builder replied. There is no evidence to support this story either.)

While work went ahead on that building site beside the Yamuna river in central India, the world was changing. The Mughal empire, though still powerful and grand, had begun an imperceptible decline which would soon become apparent. Let us pause now to see what was happening elsewhere around the world in the 1630s. It was an interesting decade.

The pilgrims who had sailed from England in the Mayflower had been in America for ten years as the decade began, and were well established — and Dutch settlers had already bought Manhattan island. The Dutch were also in Java and the Moluccas — and their sailors in Mauritius were busy clubbing the dodo into extinction. In the East Indies, a navigator named Abel Tasman was getting ready for a voyage which would take him all around mainland Australia (without actually finding it) to discover Tasmania and New Zealand. James Cook, destined to become another great navigator, was a toddler, two years old in 1630.

Peter Paul Rubens, Velazquez, Rembrandt van Rijn and van Dyck were all painting themselves famous. John Milton (in 1630) was twenty-three years old (but Shakespeare had died in 1616). Some people in England, where Oliver Cromwell had recently entered Parliament, were wondering if a new-fangled steam engine had any future. Bernini, the sculptor and architect, was the toast of Rome, where in 1633 (about the time Shah Jahan was terrorising his architects over that wooden model) Galileo Galilei went on trial in Rome for holding that the sun was the centre of the universe and that the earth revolved around it.

Before they see an acknowledged wonder of the world, most people are apt to psychologically prepare themselves for disappointment. Every visit to the Taj Mahal, however, is a new and deeper experience. As one passes through the domed hall of the portal, the Taj itself bursts into view. Appreciation is necessarily personal, but the dominant impression almost invariably is of the monument's matchless beauty and unrivalled harmony of proportion. — John Lall, in Taj Mahal and the Glory of Mughal Agra, New Delhi, 1982.

Russian explorers marching through Siberia were about to reach the Pacific, only to find their way south blocked by the new Ch'ing dynasty in Manchuria — which was all set to take over China from the native Ming rulers, and then endure until 1912. In Japan, the new Tokugawa regime was riding high, forbidding emigration and trying bloodily to eradicate Christianity, laying the foundations for rule that would last another two centuries. Europe was embroiled in the confusion of its Thirty Years' War.

What word of the outside world reached Agra is not clear. A flow of travellers and diplomatic letters to and fro would have produced some basic information. Certainly Shah Jahan and his generals were interested in any new weapons they learned about, and perhaps they were also worried by increasing numbers of European ships around India's shores. They were not as blase as Akbar was reported to be, who wondered aloud what harm a few men in boats could do.

Imrit Tana is a saddhu, and a dictionary says a saddhu is a wandering holy man. But Imrit, sixty years old, had spent twenty years almost in the shadow of the Taj Mahal when this picture was taken. A passer-by said that travelling was not essential; being holy, devoted to God, was enough.

Imrit's home is an old house, doorless and simple, under a tree on the bank of the Yamuna river just across from the Taj, amid wheatfields, vegetable gardens and ruins. He was well known and liked; he said the village policeman came to see him most mornings for a chat, and in the evenings, as in this picture, old men came to sit huddled nearby as Imrit posed for a photograph.

What did he know about the Taj? 'Shah Jahan built it to make his wife famous — what more is there to know?' he replied. Imrit and the people of the nearby village believed that Shah Jahan planned to build a black replica of the Taj as his own mausoleum on this side of the river. They pointed to surrounding brick ruins as evidence that work actually got started. It is a good story and it would have been a shame to tell them they were wrong. On the other hand, they were not wrong about the quality of those bricks. 'Very good material for building,' one said. 'It has lasted for centuries. Today's bricks will just crumble.'

As mentioned, a Portuguese intrusion in Bengal was being dealt with right at that time, but not necessarily because it represented a threat to Mughal power. If Shah Jahan and his advisers felt themselves safe from outside powers, they were right, but they were wrong if they felt themselves secure. Trouble which would eventually destroy them was right there alongside them, in Agra, even within the palace.

Meanwhile there was a monument to be built. The foundations had been completed and the design agreed on. Enormous wagons laden with marble and hauled by bullock and buffalo teams twenty and thirty strong were on their way from Makrana in Rajasthan. As mentioned earlier, the Taj Museum displays copies of orders from Shah Jahan to the local ruler who controlled Makrana telling him to send marble cutters to Makrana and to keep supplies rolling. Arrangements were made for the workers to be paid.

In Agra, there was a crisis. There was not enough timber, Shah Jahan was told, for scaffolding; use bricks and mortar, he replied, which begs more detail about how it was done, but we are not given any. Some pockmarked areas around the Taj Mahal today may date back to all that brickmaking of three centuries ago. There were undoubtedly other crises too, because no project ever goes entirely smoothly and this one was mammoth. So many workers were involved, over so many years, handling such vast quantities of material and working to such fine specifications, that only expert management could have seen it through.

We have the names of some of the expert craftsmen. Ismail Khan, possibly from Samarkand in central Asia, supervised work on the dome, building one atop the other in a method perfected earlier. Overall supervision was by Makramat Khan and Mir Abdul Karim. Designer of the gardens was Ali Mardan Khan. The Koranic calligraphy which adorns so many surfaces was by Amanat Khan from Shiraz. His name is the only one (except for those of Shah Jahan and Mumtaz Mahal on their tombs) anywhere in the Taj, in the main chamber with a date corresponding to 1639. Amanat Khan was such a clever calligrapher that he designed the script along the top of archways to be one and a quarter times the size of that at lower levels, to ensure it all looks the same. Sources and translations of the inscriptions are given in a book, Agra and Its Monuments, by B.D. Sanwal (New Delhi, 1968). Mr Sanwal was a senior official and a close student of history in Agra for many years.

Work to be done ranged from the heaviest to the finest. As we have no pictures to show the scene, we can only imagine the present Taj grounds and beyond strewn with masses of marble and bricks while thousands of men, with elephants, horses and camels to help them, hauled and chivied material into position. As the dome mounted higher, lifting slabs of marble into position must have been complicated and perilous. In shady corners artisans patiently carved marble panels and the calligraphy work, while others, the cream of all artisans present, spent months perhaps creating a single flower of gems inlaid into stone. Add to all this the chisel sharpeners, the mortar mixers and carriers, the water carriers, the messengers, the strolling overseers, the cooks in open-air kitchens all around, and the scene would have been truly kaleidoscopic.

There are records which show that master craftsmen were well paid and it may be presumed that all workers received some sort of wage. A commentary to the Taj published last century said the labour was forced and that rapacious officials stole from the workers' allowances of corn, but this seems not to tally with what is known of building practices of that age. Far from labour being forced, it may in fact have been eager to get work, much as it is today, no matter how low the pay.

As well as records which give an indication of pay scales, there are others which seem at first to give an idea of the total cost of the Taj Mahal. Even if they are reliable, and they are not, they would still be almost entirely meaningless because currency values and exchange rates have changed so much. Questions about the cost of the monument are both unanswerable and irrelevant. What is certain, so rich was the empire, is that paying the bills was no problem at all.

A French traveller said that the Taj Mahal took twenty thousand men twentytwo years to build, but this appears too symmetrical, too glib. These are the sort of figures that trip easily off the tongue but do not necessarily represent reality. Yet they do permit guides to point to the twentytwo small domes on top of the main entrance gate and say that they represent the years of construction. This seems to be nothing more than convenient conjecture.

Rather it appears that building the main monument took about ten years, with another five or so for the surroundings. Travellers' tales indicate the whole job to have been completed before 1650. Meanwhile Shah Jahan was indulging his taste for building elsewhere, especially in Delhi where he began work on Shahjahanabad in 1638.

During the years of construction and then for as long as he remained emperor, Shah Jahan if he were in Agra would observe the anniversary of Mumtaz Mahal's death with prayers in the Taj grounds. According to the ASI's guide to the Taj Museum, lofty and luxurious tents would be erected and an assembly of the greatest in the land — the powerful, the learned, the accomplished, the pious and the saintly — would recite prayers for the departed soul. At a certain stage the emperor would segregate himself and spend the night praying. Food and drink would be provided and money distributed to the needy. Similar meetings for the women of the harem and others for women in general were held later.

In time these occasions became grand indeed. The markets attached to the Taj Mahal would come into their own with fantastic displays of goods from all over Asia, from Chinese silks to Indonesian spices to Persian carpets to Sri Lankan and Burmese gems. When Shah Jahan arrived, however, he would be the centre of all attention. In his book mentioned earlier, B.D. Sanwal described what it would have been like to be there. The passage which follows is reproduced by kind permission of the author.

*Y*ou would then see the household cavalry arriving with two richly decorated elephants behind them. The cavalry would trot ahead and the elephants would advance towards the main gateway of the Taj. The emperor would dismount from his elephant and his daughters and grandsons from the other one. The royal herald would proclaim in a stentorian voice, 'Behold, the Protector of the Realm, the shadow of God on earth, the scion of the house of Timur, the second Lord of the twin conjunction, the Emperor Shah Jahan.' And you see in the distance a tall, well-built man with aquiline features, piercing eyes and a gray, closely cut and well groomed small beard. On his head is a turban slanting backwards and kept in place by pearl strings. He wears a long, close fitting robe and holds a rose in his left hand. You can see that the emperor is in poor health from his slow gait and his slight stoop. He is 63 years old.

In his eyes you can still see the fire of the house of Timur but his aspect is gentle and his whole bearing displays a singular spirit of indulgence. The blood of the ruthless Timur who ordered the slaughter of hundreds of thousands, razed innumerable cities and destroyed hundreds of petty and large principalities flows in his veins. But he is three-quarters a son of the Indian soil; both he and his father were born of Hindu Rajput princesses. He has in him both the frenzy and tumult of the Turk and the mildness and tolerance of the Indian. . . .

[The Emperor] is accompanied by his daughters, Jahanara and Roshanara, the Prime Minister and the court poet. He is followed by about a dozen members of the royal household. At the gateway, [he] pauses for a moment as he first gets a glimpse of the mausoleum that he built for his wife. His pallid countenance glows for a minute and again reverts to its usual sadness. Softly and slowly he descends the steps and goes towards the central marble reservoir. The evening shadows are falling and the Emperor sits on the marble bench and gazes at the Taj. A conversation like the following ensues:

'Jahanara, it is now twentyfive long years since you lost your mother.'

'Yes, Sire,' she replies.

'I remember vividly the last time your mother spoke to me.... [It was] when Gauhar was born. Your mother could not bear the strain and she realised the end was near. You were by her bedside and she asked you to call me immediately to her. I was in the next room but I never realised that the end was so near. It was only when I came to her bedside that I saw what was going to befall . . .

'Your mother opened her eyes when she heard me come in. She could hardly speak. I sat on her bed and held her soft hands in mine. She called all the children to her bed and said to me, "Please look after them and my parents when I am no more". She could say nothing else and tears filled her eyes. I wiped the tears away and looked into her eyes. I could not say anything to her. Speech had forsaken me. There was so much to say to her and when she was leaving me for all time I could not utter a word. And then I saw her just melt away before me . . . I only wish I could have told your mother before her death how much I loved her, and that time would prove no one ever loved a woman more than I loved your mother.'

[The architecture of the Taj Mahal] mingles with poetry and music to become an utterance of the human soul in a moment of supreme ecstacy. . . . The Taj comes as a revelation, as something that belongs to all peoples, all climates and all cultures, something that men and women have desired ever since love was born. — M. Mujeeb, in The Indian Muslims, London, 1967.

Had Mumtaz Mahal not died when she did, later events might have flowed differently. Shah Jahan might have attended more closely to the problem of succession and prevented the bloodbath which ensued as their four sons fought for the throne. The decline of the dynasty might have been delayed. As it was, the Mughal empire slid downhill to an ignominious end. Had Mumtaz Mahal lived, she might have been able to prevent her sons fighting like dogs for her husband's throne. Or the horror of losing three of them might have made her wish that she too were dead.

Shah Jahan

Before his coronation, Shah Jahan had all possible other contenders for the throne murdered in a crime of 'unparalleled hideosity', as one historian put it. He waded to the throne through blood. Perhaps some would say he had no choice. The Mughals and their ancestors in central Asia had a saying, the throne or the coffin. A society which put no faith in the rights of the first-born son, or primogeniture, had long been content to let princes fight it out, no matter how many people died in the process. It was a form of natural selection.

When Shah Jahan became emperor he and Mumtaz Mahal had four sons — Muhammad Dara Shikoh, aged thirteen; Muhammad Shuja, twelve; Muhammad Aurangzeb, ten; and Murad Baksh, four. Shah Jahan's own performance when he became emperor, not to mention his earlier revolt against his father, surely caused him to reflect that another bloody sequence was in the making — or did he look so benignly on his sons that he never imagined them ambitious and brutal? He was softening with age, and perhaps he imagined the whole world had also done so. But he had sown the seed and would reap the whirlwind.

Before then, however, he would make his mark as a splendid and brilliant ruler, generally tolerant and enlightened, and as a patron of

Four brothers fight for Shah Jahan's throne, and the empire is awash with blood. Another illustration from Valentyn's Old and New India.

the arts. Much that he did was inspired by his ambition to go into history as the greatest of the Mughals but he could not equal Akbar, his great and innovative grandfather, in social reforms, religious liberalism or military exploits. The arteries of empire were hardening too fast for similar displays of genius.

As if recognising this limitation, Shah Jahan turned to architecture as his greatest fascination. Even before the Taj Mahal was completed he was busy changing Delhi and adding his touch to buildings elsewhere throughout his vast realm. Some historians find in his delight with building an indication of what was going wrong with the empire, as if it were becoming as hard and inflexible as marble.

Early in his rule, as a corollary to building, Shah Jahan ordered construction of what would certainly be the world's most flamboyant item of furniture. His 'peacock throne', when it was eventually installed in the Agra Fort, was nearly three metres long, more than two metres wide and and nearly five metres high, totally adorned with gold and jewels. The towering canopy was mounted on twelve emerald columns, with the images of two peacocks on top of each column. Between each pair of peacocks was a tree set with rubies, diamonds, emeralds and pearls.

'So valuable and adorned a throne was never seen in any other age,' wrote a traveller at the time. Shah Jahan first used it in 1635. Later it

Previous pages — Shah Jahan holds court, apparently in the open air. In this unusual and colourful two-page rendering, he is shown on the right accepting a gift of pearls from his prime minister, Asaf Khan (Mumtaz Mahal's father). Courtiers, almost all shown in profile, look on respectfully.

In the left-hand picture, musicians, dancing girls appear to be waiting to put on a show — along with an elephant and two horses. The women, being without veils, must be of lowly status; no noblewoman would appear thus in the company for men. The picture on the right has

been described as showing Shah Jahan on the peacock throne but the jewelled peacocks and trees of that throne are not visible here. Perhaps they are hidden behind the canopies. But the throne is certainly lavish and ornate. Shah Jahan's beard is said to have turned white when Mumtaz Mahal died. Here it is dark. But the peacock throne did not exist in Mumtaz's time. Perhaps his beard turned black again. Perhaps the portrait is a copy of an earlier one. Perhaps the artist felt he should not depict his emperor as an old man. — Reproduced by permission of the Trustees of the British Museum.

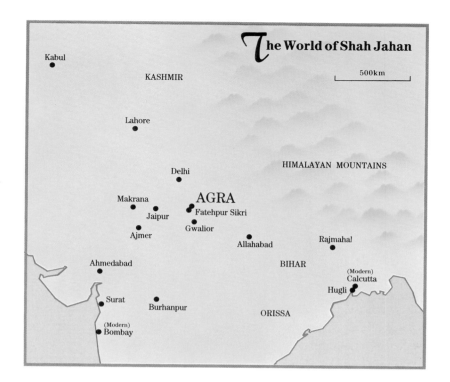

The World of Shah Jahan

Kabul

KASHMIR

500km

Lahore

HIMALAYAN MOUNTAINS

Delhi

AGRA

Makrana
Jaipur   Fatehpur Sikri
Ajmer   Gwalior
           Allahabad   Rajmahal

Ahmedabad   BIHAR
                                (Modern)
                                Calcutta
                         Hugli

Surat
    Burhanpur   ORISSA

(Modern)
Bombay

was moved to Delhi, where less than a century later invading Persians included it in their loot and took it home. They treated it with less than honour, however, mining it for its riches and breaking it up. Now only the legend remains, along with some not very convincing paintings done by artists who could never have seen the original.

As well as building, Shah Jahan fought. In mediaeval India, according to Muni Lal, the job of minor rulers was to hunt, to honour the dead past and to resist paying taxes and tribute to the imperial power; and one of the jobs of the imperial power was to wage wars to bring minor rulers back to the path of obedience. Imperial armies marched here and there on such police actions until Shah Jahan — perhaps still hoping to excel Akbar as a soldier — decided on campaigns in central Asia. He threw in army after army, only to learn later of crushing defeats. If the Taj Mahal is his monument to love, his vain battles were monuments to his indifference to life.

Some travellers at that time wrote that his failures so depressed Shah Jahan that he turned to fleshly pleasures for consolation. A persistent but unproven story is that he had an incestuous relationship with his oldest daughter Jahanara, who had taken over the role of first lady of the empire when Mumtaz Mahal died. Whatever the truth, it is certain that Jahanara became increasingly important in his life — perhaps as one of the few people he could trust. She became a model of filial loyalty, a fixed point around which all else in the palace revolved. Shah Jahan had other wives but none ever took the place of Mumtaz Mahal in his heart.

Jahanara never married and stayed with her father to the end. Why she did not marry is not known but a likely explanation lies in the difficulty Shah Jahan would have found in getting her an acceptable husband. Men could 'marry down' without disgracing themselves or their families but women could not. A suitable match for Jahanara would have to be of her own rank — and there was none such. She could not even be married to another king, perhaps as a political gesture, as this would raise her husband to near her father's level, and that Shah Jahan would not do.

In 1644 Jahanara came near death when a lamp set her dress on fire. Two of her slaves were fearfully burned as they beat out the flames, one of them dying later, and Jahanara also lay near death for four months. It is a sidelight on history that among the doctors called to treat her was a Mr Gabriel Boughton, who was then in Surat, an English East India Company settlement north of modern Bombay. When his daughter had recovered, Shah Jahan invited Boughton to name his own reward. He could have emerged rich, but instead he asked for trading privileges for his company throughout the empire. India would have fallen to the English anyway but Boughton's action certainly helped.

In 1657 Shah Jahan, then over sixty, fell ill and rumours spread that he had died. His four sons were in their posts as imperial governors in Allahabad, Rajmahal, Burhanpur and Ahmedabad — all well away from the capital. The oldest son, Dara Shikoh, a capable and popular prince, had been named heir to the throne but the other three each decided to try for it. Perhaps they felt they had no choice, because tradition was that the winner would murder his brothers.

What happened next was not just a palace feud with duels and backstabbings. The brothers, as heads of great provinces, fielded huge armies which engaged in bloody battles. Hundreds of thousands of men were caught up in this family squabble and tens of thousands of them died. Briefly, Dara beat Shuja but then was defeated in a monumental conflict by Aurangzeb and Murad fighting together. Aurangzeb turned on Murad and Shuja, beat them both and emerged victorious from the shambles. It was no less than Auranzeb felt he deserved, because he was determined, single-minded and fanatical with Islamic zeal. He saw himself as doing God's work.

But Shah Jahan was not dead. He had recovered from his illness and was watching in horror. 'I am puzzled by the difference between you and your brothers,' he wrote to Dara, supporting him. 'Mumtaz gave birth to all of you. How is it that from your pores oozes out honey and from theirs the bitterest poison?' Just how poisonous the austere and humourless Aurangzeb in particular was he was soon to learn.

Dara, the first born son, the favoured one, the heir to the throne, after his first defeat, was harried half across India, beaten again and again in vain stands, until he was betrayed, captured and sent to Delhi in chains. Filthy, wretched and mounted on an equally filthy

From a chapter of the Arabian Nights, from the middle of the most gorgeous fairy tale the mind of man could invent, I write to you tonight. Often have I heard of the Taj Mahal, read of its beauty, dreamed of its magic, but never in my dreams did I imagine anything so exquisite, so perfect. . . . I am no more capable of describing it than I would have been of building it; you must see it for yourself. It alone is worth coming to India to see.
— A young Englishwoman, Olivia Douglas, to her fiance in England.

elephant, he was paraded through the streets, humiliated, imprisoned and beheaded.

Shuja, all hope lost, fled east to Dacca, in present-day Bangladesh, and thence to Arakan in modern Burma. His followers deserted him one by one as he moved further into what was for them barbaric territory. A bloodthirsty chief turned on what had become a pathetic expedition. Amid the turmoil Shuja slipped away into the jungle, where he was probably killed by primitive tribesmen.

Murad was captured in a conspiracy which involved pretty women and wine, bound and taken on an emaciated elephant to Delhi, to undergo just such humiliation as Dara's. He was jailed, and then moved to Gwalior, east of Agra, for incarceration in one of the most feared prisons in India. A charge of murder was rigged against him, he was found guilty, and executed.

Meanwhile, Shah Jahan had moved from Delhi to Agra, so, it was said, that if he died from his illness he would do so within sight of the tomb of his beloved Mumtaz Mahal. Recovering, and learning that his sons were already manoeuvring to seize the throne, he wrote letters urging them to abandon confrontation and to restore family unity. It was all in vain. Aurangzeb had been plotting for years to become emperor and was not to be stopped.

In June, 1658, Aurangzeb entered Agra. Shah Jahan found himself isolated in the Fort with a garrison of about two thousand men. A siege began. Shah Jahan continued to plead for a solution, proposing that the empire be divided between the brothers while Aurangzeb ruled in Agra as the fount of supreme authority. This was rejected because Aurangzeb saw himself as fulfilling a God-given role. 'It is not that I love you less but that I love Islam more,' he would write to his father later. Such dedication soon produced entry into the Fort. Further resistance was pointless. Shah Jahan became his son's prisoner.

Aurangzeb turned his attention to dealing with Dara, arranging his capture, humiliation and death, as mentioned earlier. That was not all. Dara's head was put in a silver casket and sent as 'a gift from the gods' to Shah Jahan. Jahanara, totally unaware, opened the casket, and screamed. Shah Jahan fell unconscious and, upon reviving, spent three days in prayer. Meanwhile Roshanara, the second daughter of Shah Jahan and Mumtaz Mahal, as fanatical as her brother Aurangzeb, held a feast and distributed money to celebrate Dara's death.

Money alone could not wash the blood away, however, as Aurangzeb learned when he invited to Delhi the man who had betrayed and captured Dara, an Afghan named Malik Jivan. Two thousand men were assigned to escort him through the streets to the Fort. But not even this show of force could prevent the people pelting him with dirt, old shoes and animal dung, or prevent men and women on their rooftops singing traditional songs which condemned treachery. Aurangzeb was furious but dared not do anything.

Dara's execution, writes Muni Lal, marked the end of the greatness of the Mughals. 'The fearless heroism of Babar, the wide and deep humanism of Humayun, the liberal tolerance of Akbar and the splendrous benevolence of Jahangir and Shah Jahan' were lost and what remained, under Aurangzeb, was 'a cobweb of enmities, jealousies, racial prejudices, extreme forms of religious fanaticism, degenerated nobility, devaluation of the arts and sciences and . . . a cupboard full of skeletons.'

Shah Jahan, emperor become prisoner, lived on and on, in a small section of the Agra Fort, for seven long years. At first he was in danger. His food was tasted to ensure it was not poisoned — and a drink prepared for him, snatched from his hand at the last moment, turned out to be lethal. It was tried on a dog, which quickly convulsed and died. His letters were read by Aurangzeb's agents. Servants were forbidden on pain of death from carrying messages, written or oral, to or from the former emperor. He lived in comfort, with women, musicians, servants and the loving Jahanara to attend to his needs, but the change from power and freedom was not an easy one.

Shah Jahan found part of his answer in religion, even if it were only to write long, complaining letters to Aurangzeb, who replied in kind. Both men sought to use passages from the Koran and other religious writing to make their cases, but there could not be a meeting of minds between father and son. The correspondence faded away into stalemate and silence. Aurangzeb got on with the job of running the empire he had taken over so bloodily, a task he performed with diminishing success. Though he ruled for more than forty years, he destroyed rather than built, and his legacy was an empire in steep and irreversible decline.

In January, 1666, Shah Jahan, seventyfour and ailing, felt his time had come. 'In a few days I shall be no more,' he is said to have told Jahanara. 'Mumtaz came to me in a dream and asked with tears rolling down her cheeks that I express a firm desire to be laid to rest by her side. . . . Heed her wish. This is my last will and testament. Throw me to the vultures if Aurangzeb does not agree.'

He was a long time dying, however. For two more weeks he lingered, sometimes conscious, sometimes in agony from an emergency operation, sometimes in a coma, until just before nightfall on January 22. He awakened from a doze and asked Jahanara to have his bed carried to an adjoining balcony overlooking the Yamuna river. There, wrapped in blankets against the chill evening air, he looked for the last time upon the monument he had built for his Mumtaz Mahal, gleaming in the last rays of the sunset. And he died.

The next morning saw a small funeral procession from the Fort to a boat which carried Shah Jahan's body down the Yamuna to the Taj Mahal, where it was carried in through a small gate at the water's edge (long since closed). The governor of Agra had banned the traditional scattering of coins to the poor from over the body of a ruler. 'A state prisoner cannot be honoured in that way,' his decree said. Jahanara defied him, throwing out a handful of silver coins as the body left the Fort.

The ceremony inside the Taj Mahal was simple. As sections of the Koran were recited, Shah Jahan's body was lowered into its grave. Earth was shovelled over it. Later workmen would arrive to build the inlaid marble tomb which visitors see today, right next to the one in which Mumtaz Mahal had been buried more than thirty years before. They had been long apart, but now they would be together for ever.

$\mathcal{A}$s children see it

The children of Kachhpura see the Taj Mahal every day of their lives. Their village stands only a kilometre away, across the Yamuna river, and they get a much better view of it, without walls to get in the way, than people who live much nearer on the south bank. What, we wondered, would happen if we asked children in the village school to draw the Taj?

With the approval and assistance of the headmaster, Mr Jagdish Prasad Verma, we distributed paper and crayons and a week later returned to see the

results, some of which are shown here. One remarkable outcome was that many of the children chose to depict the Taj not as they see it but as tourists do — not from their side of the river but from inside the main gate.

To make the event more interesting, we turned it into a competition, with prizes for the best work by girls and boys. The winning girls were Afaroj Begam, ten years old, Mithilesh Kunari, nine, and Mamata Devi, nine. The boys who won prizes were Vijnesh Kumar, ten, Sajjan Kumar Sagar, nine, and Sohan Lal Sagar, eight.

Kacchpura village, where people at present make their livings mainly as farmers or leather workers, lies within the area marked for development as the Taj Mahal national park. Planners say these and other villagers affected will be integrated into the economy of the park, but how this will be done is not yet known.

Six of the drawings are shown on these pages and there is another, small, on page 109. Above, children during the judging.

TAJ MAHAL

142

143

Not just the Taj Mahal

Long before Shah Jahan met Mumtaz Mahal, Agra was famous. This chapter will trace its history and deal in particular with four of the 'other monuments' of that Agra Cantonment railway station sign which invites tourists to alight to see the Taj Mahal: Agra Fort, Fatehpur Sikri, Akbar's tomb at Sikandra, and the tomb of Itmad-ud-Daula — the immediate forerunner of the Taj

Agra's existence can be traced back to the almost mythical times of the Mahabharata, the great Indian epic. Krishna, the most celebrated of Hindu deities, is said to have been born in Mathura, only forty kilometres away, home now to a big oil refinery. The region, including Agra itself, is rich with archaeological remains which attest to flourishing Brahman, Buddhist and Jain communities.

When Muslim invasions from Persia and Afghanistan began in the Eighth Century, it was soon perceived that control of Delhi and Agra brought with it control of most of north India. This was especially so when a Muslim power ruled Agra and when the Hindu Rajputs of Jaipur were determined they should come no further. It was as if these early Muslim invaders and their Hindu foes were laying down the rules for the formidable onslaught that was about to break over all of them. Agra was to be a centre of foreign military supremacy, Jaipur an Indian bulwark against it.

Agra's historic buildings and sites offer much to see — not all of it historic. This picture, left, was taken in Fatehpur Sikri.

Not that the arrival of the Mughals seemed all that momentous at first — just bloody. In 1398 Tamerlane rode in from central Asia, sacked Delhi, raised pyramids of human heads, and rode out again. Five generations later his descendant Babar used artillery, ingenious calvalry tactics and astounding nerve to take both Delhi and Agra.

Babar was larger than life. Descended on his father's side from

Humayun

Tamurlane and on his mother's from Genghis Khan, he brought astonishing zest to everything he did. His career was scored with brilliant victories, defeats, flights, recoveries, betrayals and then victories once more. But he was not just a determined soldier. He was a statesman, a poet, a diarist, a lover of flowers who created gardens wherever he went, including one in Agra — but probably not the one called Ram Bagh which is often attributed to him. Babar's garden was further south and only traces remain. Ram Bagh, in such disrepair now as to be hardly worth visiting, was probably made by one of his nobles; its Hindu-sounding name came in the Eighteenth Century when Hindu Mahrattas occupied Agra. Babar died in Agra in 1530 and his body was taken to Kabul for burial.

(Babar and the later Mughals preferred not to be called Mughals. They saw themselves as Timurids, descendants of Tamerlane, and are said to have regarded the Mongols — whence we get the word Mughal — as rabble horsemen of the steppes.)

Babar's son Humayun took over the nascent empire, promptly lost it, and had to be helped back to power by a wily Persian king who saw something in it for himself. All accounts agree that Humayun, whose tomb is one of the great sights of Delhi, was a pleasant, well intentioned and earnest man; but he has gone into history mainly as the father of the next Mughal emperor, Akbar, the greatest of them all.

If Babar was a hero of action, Akbar was a hero of the mind. Not that he avoided action. There was no greater soldier in his day, and it took genius to turn his ramshackle inheritance into the great empire which he left to later generations. But he brought to the job of ruling it an intelligence, a sense of humanity and a generosity of spirit which emblazon his reign with glory.

Akbar left his mark on Agra even more surely than Shah Jahan did, and for a time the town was known as Akbarabad. He built the huge Agra Fort, with red stone walls more than twenty metres high and noble gateways, on the site of an old Hindu castle. He made it his seat of government for most of his reign. His son Jahangir and grandson Shah Jahan added much to it and it is a grand place today, though reduced to its bare bones. The visitor who tries to imagine it as it must have been will have his imagination well rewarded. Here is a description of how part of it might have been by E.B. Havell, the writer on Indian art and achitecture already much quoted in this book:

Babar

'When the afterglow fills the sky, burnishes the gilded roofs, and turns the marble to rose, imagination may re-people these lovely pavilions with fair Indian women — revel in the feast of colour in saris, brocades and carpets; in the gold, azure and crimson of the painted ceilings; and listen to the water splashing in the fountains and gurgling over the carved water-shoots — a scene of voluptuous beauty such as the world has rarely known.'

And here is another description, this one by the French doctor Francois Bernier, written more than three hundred years ago, which applies as well to the Mughal court in Agra as it did to Delhi, where he saw these sights:

'The monarch every day, about noon, sits upon his throne, with some of his sons to his right and left, while eunuchs standing about the royal person flap away the flies with peacocks' tails, agitate the air with large fans, or wait with undivided attention and profound humility to perform the different services allotted to each. [Nobles, rajahs and ambassadors stand in a special enclosure while] the remainder of the spacious room, and, indeed, the whole courtyard, is filled with persons of all ranks, high and low, rich and poor; because it is in this extensive hall that the king gives audience indiscriminately to all his subjects . . .

'During the hour and a half, or two hours, that this ceremony continues, a certain number of the royal horses pass before the throne, that the king may see that they are well used and in a proper condi-

Humayun's tomb in Delhi, heavy and hugging the ground, is a forerunner to the light and ethereal Taj Mahal.

tion. The elephants come next, their filthy hides having been well washed and painted black as ink, with two large red streaks from the top of the head down to the trunk, where they meet. The elephants are covered with embroidered cloth; a couple of silver-white cow-tails from Great Tibet, of large value, hang from their ears like immense whiskers . . .

'As if proud of his gorgeous attire and of the magnificence which surrounds him, each elephant moves with a solemn and dignified step, and, when in front of the throne, the driver, who is seated on his shoulder, pricks him with a pointed iron, animates and speaks to him, until the animal bends one knee, lifts his trunk on high and roars aloud . . .

'Other animals are next introduced — tame antelopes, kept for the purpose of fighting with each other; nilgaux, or grey oxen, that appear to me to be a species of elk; rhinoceroses; large Bengal buffaloes, with prodigious horns which enable them to contend against lions and tigers; tame leopards, or panthers, employed in hunting antelopes; some of the fine sporting dogs from Uzbek . . .'

Much of the Agra Fort today is occupied by the army — as it was, obviously, in Mughal times, and then British — but much remains open for the visitor to see. He is free to wander through courtyards

Of all the tombs which one sees at Agra, that of the wife of Shah Jahan is the most splendid. He purposely made it near the Tasimacan, where all foreigners come, so that the whole world should see and admire its magnificence. The Tasimacan is a large bazaar, consisting of six large courts all surrounded with porticoes, under which there are chambers for the use of merchants, and an enormous quantity of cottons is sold there. The tomb of this Begum, or sultan queen, is at the east end of the town by the side of the river in a great square surrounded by walls. . . . From time to time [the tomb attendants] change the carpet, chandeliers and other ornaments of that kind, and there are always there some Mollahs to pray. I witnessed the commencement and accomplishment of this great work, on which they have expended twentytwo years, during which twenty thousand men worked incessantly; this is sufficient to enable one to realise that the cost of it has been enormous. — Jean Baptiste Tavernier, Travels in India, 1676. (Tavernier, a jeweller, spent years in Agra from 1641 onwards. It seems impossible that he saw work begin.)

and compartments, the halls of public and private audience, the high terrace with its slabs of black and white marble which served as thrones, and the former harem. Shah Jahan and Mumtaz Mahal lived here for three years after he became emperor. After her death, he continued to spend much time here — ruling directly from the newly installed peacock throne. And after he was overthrown by his son Aurangzeb he was imprisoned here, in an elevated, airy suite of rooms with the Taj Mahal in full view across the river. There was much to remind him of Mumtaz.

Particularly interesting is the contrast between parts where the architecture in red stone is powerfully Hindu, from Akbar's times, and parts in white marble which reflect Shah Jahan's different style. Jahangir's palace, despite its name, was probably built mainly by Akbar and is extraordinary in its robust decorations. Shah Jahan

added buildings of white marble which are just as memorable for their delicacy and style. His Pearl Mosque in particular has been described as achieving its stunning effect solely by the perfection of its proportions, beauty of material and harmony of design.

The Fort contains also, barely visible behind glass, evidence of a scholarly blunder. A British governor general, Lord Ellenborough, sought to win favour with Indians by celebrating the return of two big wooden gates seized during an expedition into Afghanistan. He thought they were the gates of a famous Hindu temple at Somnath taken away by invaders more than six hundred years before. They

were paraded ceremoniously through town after town across north India and then installed with still more ceremony in the Agra Fort.

The only problem was that they were not the Somnath gates, being of the wrong material and design. 'One glance would convince any expert on Oriental archaeology,' Havell commented sourly later, 'that they could not by any possibility have been the gates of a Hindu temple.' But they are still in the Fort, as if no one knows what to do with them.

Remarkable though the Agra Fort is, it pales beside another Akbar creation, Fatehpur Sikri, twentythree kilometres from Agra. The story is that Akbar consulted a holy man living there about his failure

Agra Fort's hall of private audience and, right, a view of the Taj Mahal from the Fort in British times, when it served as an armoury.

to get a son and heir. The holy man advised him to live nearby — and nine months later a son, Jahangir, the future emperor, was born. Akbar was so impressed that he decided to make his capital there, and a new city arose at his command.

In its day it was a splendid place, and today, though only the stones remain, it is still to be savoured. This is more easily done if you are lucky enough to have a guide who explains that in its heyday the palace was strewn and hung with carpets and tapestries, that the empty doorways had doors, and that the now spartan courtyards

were covered with bright canopies — the hooks to support them can still be seen.

Much remains of a city wall eight kilometres long, nine metres high, more than two metres wide, and pierced by nine gateways. The wall surrounded the city on three sides and a man-made lake protected the fourth. Within, it is hard to say which is the outstanding attraction. Here are a few words about some of them.

The Panch Mahal ('panch' means five and the building is five storeys high) towers over everything else. Originally each storey would have been enclosed in pierced stone screens, and as it over-

Two views of Fatehpur Sikri, an astonishing complex which Akbar created, used as his capital for seventeen years, and abandoned. The building above is the Panch Mahal.

looked the harem area it is virtually certain that it could have been used only by Akbar and the women of his court. Its main purpose was to catch cool breezes in mid-summer.

The 'Turkish sultan's palace' probably was never just one woman's palace. This small building with almost every inch of its stone walls and ceilings elegantly carved (and with some carvings of animals mutilated by iconoclastic Muslims) is more likely to have been the place where Akbar's wife for the night waited to be taken across the yard to his private quarters. (Women of his court also at times had to serve as living, moving pieces on a large parchisi board laid out in the middle of the courtyard.)

The hall of private audience is a kind of debating chamber in which Akbar would have taken his seat on a highly ornamented column with bridges linking it to each corner of the room. Dignitaries would have waited at the ends of the bridges and on the floor below. The ambience is impressive — especially as it was here that Akbar debated the nature of religion and attempted to devise a common creed for all his subjects. He did not succeed but the attempt was honourable and he is highly regarded for it in India even today.

Another courtyard nearby has a towering gateway, the Baland Darwaza, the highest in India, taller than the Arc de Triomphe. Inside the courtyard there is an impressive mosque and a charming, white marble shrine holding the tomb of the holy man, Shaikh Salim Chisti, who advised Akbar on how to go about getting a son. It is a place of pilgrimage for many people.

Akbar maintained his court at Fatepur Sikri from 1568 to 1586, when he moved it back to Agra. Agra was no doubt pleased when all those courtiers, officials, soldiers and traders brought themselves and their families and servants back and revived its languid economy. Fatehpur Sikri was abandoned to the jungle, and soon after an English traveller would write, 'Ruin all; lying like a waste desert, and very dangerous to pass through in the night.'

It is now known why Akbar so abandoned his creation. The commonest explanation is that it ran out of water but an emperor with

Three generations of Mughal power in one painting — Emperor Akbar meets his son Jahangir (in red turban) and his grandson Prince Khurram, the future Shah Jahan, then a child with curly side locks. More than a century of imperial power is represented in this one picture. Reproduction is by permission of the Metropolitan Museum of Art, New York, gift of Alexander Smith Cochran, 1913.

the resources to build Fatehpur Sikri in the first place should have been able also to divert a river or two. A more likely reason is that political and military developments demanded that he move to a more central position. Perhaps he felt isolated out there? An explanation which can be seriously doubted is that the holy man came to him one day and said the place had become too crowded. 'One of us will have to leave,' he declared. So Akbar decided to go. If you believe that you will believe every other story you hear in India as well.

Akbar died in 1605 (two years after Queen Elizabeth I of England, whose career, as noted earlier, coincided closely with Akbar's). Before he died he had begun work on his own monument north of Agra. It was at a place called Sikandra (in English, Alexandria), and even the name acts as an historical trigger. It was named after Sultan Sikander Lodi, who made Agra his capital— and whose son Ibrahim was beaten by Babar in a pivotal battle near Delhi in 1526. When Akbar chose Sikandra for his tomb, without bothering to change the name, was he thumbing his nose at a dynasty which thought it could resist the Mughals? Or was he conceding that in death all men are equal?

Just as he had done with Agra Fort and at Fatehpur Sikri, Akbar built his monument on a huge scale. The area marked off for it covers sixty hectares and the walls around it are nearly two and a half kilometres long and more than seven metres high. Four towering gateways (three of them 'blind', just for symmetry and effect, and one actually in use) loom above the surrounding plain and attract the attention of travellers on the Taj Express.

The mausoleum set in the centre of this area stands on a white marble platform one hundred metres square and is five storeys high — the lowest of them nine metres high, with towers at each corner. Beyond this the structure goes up and up, and some see in it similarities to the Panch Mahal at Fatehpur Sikri. The topmost level, where stands a replica of Akbar's tombstone in a gloomy vault far below, has no roof, as if it were his wish 'that light and air could come to him from the four corners of the universe'.

The phrase is B.D. Sanwal's, from his excellent Agra and its Monuments, which tells how Akbar, the grandson and son of foreigners, decided to establish the family permanently in India by marrying Rajput princesses and giving Rajputs and other Indians his confidence and some of the highest offices of state. 'Such treatment of non-believers was unheard of in those days,' Sanwal continues, 'and every Indian today remembers with admiration Akbar who in the Sixteenth

Century maintained . . . that every Indian was equal and could rise to the highest positions in art, literature, the army and the services of the state.'

Some historians have written that Jahangir, left to complete the monument after his father's death, changed it in some details and left it unfinished in others. Havell, writing around the turn of this century, said the structure gave the idea of a noble but uncompleted idea. 'Both in its greatness and its uncompleteness, it is typical of Akbar and his works,' he said. This is an engaging notion, but it seems now to be accepted that the building is much as Akbar intended.

Back in Agra, on the bank of the Yamuna river opposite and upstream from the Fort, stands another remarkable mausoleum, more modest and more elegant. It contains the remains of Jahangir's prime minister, who had the title Itmad-ud-Daulah, and thus it is generally known. His wife is buried there too, and other members of their family. Now, however, the memorial is seen less as a tribute to the people buried there than to the woman who created it.

She was Nur Jahan, wife of Jahangir, daughter of Itmad-ud-Daulah, and a force in her own right in the India of her times. Her career has already been outlined in this book, because as Mumtaz Mahal's aunt she was involved in delaying Mumtaz's marriage to Shah Jahan and also in a conspiracy to prevent Shah Jahan becoming emperor. These instances make her appear grim, but in a fairer world it would be she and not Mumtaz who is best remembered. Poor Mumtaz without the Taj Mahal would have been long forgotten, or remembered only as just another imperial wife.

Nur Jahan fought her way out of that stew and by courage and intelligence became a power in the land. Her husband Jahangir helped by being often drunk and distracted from his work, so that a vacuum existed for Nur Jahan to fill, but by any reading she was extraordinary. As mentioned earlier, Kanwar Lal, a careful writer, describes her as 'one of the most beautiful, cultured, elegant, gracious, gifted, taste-endowed and talented queens in world history'. Her parents' memorial is also her own.

It is small, by the standards of the time, but exceedingly elegant, notable for its perfect proportions and for the inlaid and mosaic ornamentation which covers most of its outer walls. It has been described as a painting executed in three dimensions, and as a jewel box, and its walls as like Persian carpets. Many visitors, especially if they felt overwhelmed by Agra's other offerings, find the result pleasing. Guides have a habit of referring to it as 'Baby Taj', which seems unfair to both buildings but which may be the only answer to difficulties in pronouncing 'Itmad-ud-Daula'. We are lucky that 'Taj Mahal' rolls so easily off the tongue.

A direct line of descent connects not just the Mughals but also their monuments. They took an architecture which had already evolved in India, partly Hindu, partly Islamic, and gave it a spirit of its own which visitors today can still appreciate.

Humayun's tomb in Delhi is a huge pile which seems to hug the earth just as the Taj Mahal seems to soar above it. But it has the octagonal design, the double dome, the lofty arches and two apparently locally developed devices, domed kiosks with projecting eaves and flower-topped pinnacles, which were to become characteristic of Mughal architecture. It even has stubby towers at each corner of the main building which were to develop into the Taj Mahal's graceful minarets. Much in the Humayun's tomb formula was applied to the construction of Fatehpur-Sikri and, later, Akbar's mausoleum, which was finished about 1613.

The Itmad-ud-Daula monument probably began life as a pleasure palace which its owner knew would eventually become his mausoleum — there was a Mughal tradition to this effect. Building it would have used both skills and artisans from the construction of Fatehpur Sikri and the Akbar mausoleum. When Nur Jahan set about converting it to its present form, in the 1620s, she was able to employ another development from Sikandra.

Builders there had learned to lay marble into the red sandstone which Akbar so loved. At the Itmad-ud-Daula monument they reversed this, laying stone of all kinds into marble. The lessons they learned, and the subtlety of their designers, were to make possible the superb inlay work of the Taj Mahal.

When Shah Jahan began casting about for ideas for the most beautiful monument the world has ever seen, everything was ready for him. All that was needed was genius to bring it all together.

The tomb of Itmad-ud-Daula, 'a painting in three dimensions,' completed shortly before work began in the Taj Mahal.

Islamic or Indian?

Some people are not content to admire the Taj Mahal for what it is. They want to label it either as a product of Indian culture or of Islamic culture. Their arguments at times become almost desperate as they seek to prove that this element or that in the Taj derives from within India or from beyond its borders. For example, there is a writer who insists that the arched niche, much in evidence in the Taj, derives from West Asia — and there is another who insists that the niche is what was left when iconoclasts pulled Hindu deities from their places in temple walls. But people who have studied the issue closely generally find a synthesis of the two cultures. Here are some examples:

Persian influences can be seen in the articulation of the facade, but in all other details, the rounding of the corners, the contour of the dome, the form of the four flanking corner towers, and in the finish of the interior, the Indian note sets the key. — Ernst Kuhnel, for many years professor of Islamic art and archaeology at the University of Berlin, in Islamic Art and Architecture, London, 1966.

The evolutionary process had already been set in motion and important monuments existed when the Mughals took over the country. They did not begin on a clean slate but gave the mediaeval architecture of India a new orientation, outlook and spirit. . . . The

Taj Mahal marks the stage of perfection in the evolution of Mughal architecture, the stage where the art could only, and in fact did, decline. . . . Some historians seek to connect the Taj with the religion and methodology of Islam. This is only a subjective view. . . . The Taj Mahal could only have been built in India and nowhere else. . . . Indo-Islamic architecture is a triumph of two great traditions. — Saryu Doshi (ed), The Age of Splendour — Islamic Art in India, Bombay, 1983.

The Taj is neither a Hindu nor an Islamic . . . building. It is the culmination of the Mughal style of architecture even as the Mughal style of architecture itself is the culmination of the process of synthesis of the Hindu tradition and the Islamic or Persian or Afghan or Turkish of the Middle East. — Kanwar Lal, The Taj, New Delhi, 1965. The book goes on to quote another writer, Goetz, as saying the Taj is 'Indian in sentiment — since it is airy and light and ethereal and subtle and fragile-looking rather than solid and strong as the traditional Muslim architecture was'.

The Taj also marks the culmination of the Mughal building art. Persian elements . . . predominate in its scheme, but the general structural idiom is essentially Indian, i.e. Mughal, for it is a logical development of the Akbari style. The Persian or central

Asian traits of the Taj are, therefore, a derivation from the buildings raised by Akbar and not a direct borrowing from Iran or central Asia. — M.C. Joshi, Is the Taj Unique in Design?, in (Indian) Science Today, October, 1973. (Mr Joshi is now joint director general of the Archaeological Survey of India.)

This Indo-Persian gem is the ultimate expression of the syncretic Indian genius which was sedulously cultivated by the greatest of the Mughals. — John Lall, Taj Mahal and the Glory of Mughal Agra, New Delhi, 1982.

The Taj Mahal is in fact exactly just such a building as one would expect to be created in India . . . by a ruler with the wealth of India at his disposal. — E.B. Havell, Ancient and Mediaeval Architecture of India, Calcutta, 1915.

[The Mughal rulers] did not comb- ine to develop a 'Mughal pattern', nor is there any evidence to show that much foreign cultural influ- ence had anything to do with the architecture which flourished under the patronage of the Mughals. On the contrary, it was a purely Indian architectural movement, wherein both the Hindu and Mohammedan crafts- men joined together their invent- ive and artistic faculties to create dreams in marble and stone. — Shanti Swarup, Arts and Crafts of India and Pakistan, Bombay, 1957.

Taking Leave

Like every other Indian city, Agra has had lots of ups and downs. In centuries past the main reasons for downs were marauding armies; and an occasional reason was an imperial decision to move the court elsewhere. A flavour of it all, good times and bad, comes not only from the Taj Mahal and the other monuments listed in the previous chapter but also from numerous other remains which bestrew the city. A map of Agra in the Seventeen Century shows upper class residences lining the river from the Taj Mahal to the Fort, and for more than a kilometre further north. Beyond this strip the city had nearly as many gateways, places of worship (including a church), tombs, cemeteries and monuments even then ancient as it had places of business and residence.

More ruins, present and future, have arisen since those days, though many of today's buildings are not going to withstand any serious test of time. Perhaps the difference is in the mortar? Even a garrison cemetery from British times in the Agra Cantonment, not so old, is crumbling into the ground. It is an evocative place particularly for the children buried there more than a hundred years ago.

One poor mite is recorded in these terms: 'Motherless, within four days of birth; sinless, I depart this earth.' Eva Emma Julia Wells lived one year, ten months and twenty days; Robert Henry Spencer, one

Newlyweds from Gwalior pose for a honeymoon picture in a setting which has come to represent romance.

Not only the monuments are interesting. The countryside abounds with colour and spectacle.

year and five months; Anne O'Connor, one year and eight months; Francis James Cameron, two years and six months, Joseph Cubbins, fifteen days; and Mary Louise Bonnard 'fell asleep' at the age of one year and twentyfour days. A tiny grave bears the inscription, 'This lovely bud so young and fair, Called hence by early doom, Just came to show how sweet a flower, In Paradise could bloom.'

Their elders died just as pathetically, from 'jungle fever', of cholera, in action during the Mutiny, 'while playing polo,' of 'heat apoplexy'. A grieving husband inscribed a stone which sits in the dust

today, announcing that 'My beloved is gone down into His garden to gather lilies'.

The British came to India as the Mughals did, as outsiders. Mughal parents surely suffered similar heartbreak on just as massive a scale — poor Mumtaz lost half her fourteen children — but they left no inscribed gravestones as the British did. You had to be a famous or wealthy Mughal to warrant a tomb. Children did not. Not many visitors find their way to that garrison cemetery, and of those who do most who were merely curious emerge curiously sad. It is a counter-point to the Taj Mahal.

Today, were it not for the Taj Mahal, Agra would be no different from dozens of other Indian cities in its appearance and in its problems.

Through the 1970s and 1980s it came under pressure from industrial development, acute population growth and rising expectations. All services — electricity, water, street maintenance, drainage, housing — have been under strain and there is no evidence that the strain will diminish. Statistically living standards have risen but the quality of life has fallen, even with the cleaner air which has resulted from campaigns to protect the Taj Mahal.

The city has a population of more than a million growing by ten percent a year, a rate which makes it difficult for the city managers to

get ahead. Time and again their schemes have been overtaken by pressure of people moving in from the villages in search of jobs and bright lights. The politics of democracy and legal process make it almost impossible to demolish buildings once they have been erected. Where land is needed for municipal purposes, court action by just one landowner can delay progress for years.

Only once in recent years has dramatic action been possible. At a time when the constitution was suspended, a VIP from Delhi found Mahatma Gandhi Road, an important tourist route which runs through the city from the Delhi road to the Cantonment, congested. Widen it, he ordered, and landowners on both sides could only watch as the bulldozers went to work. Now the road is wider and straighter — but congested once more.

An important tool in official attempts to improve Agra is the Agra Development Authority, one of twentysix like it in the state of Uttar Pradesh. Founded in 1974 and with a staff of two hundred and fifty, mostly engineers, it concentrates on developing housing, office and shopping areas, on widening streets and installing street lights, and on 'beautification', especially tree planting. As mentioned earlier, the authority derives part of its revenue from its three-quarters share of

Market scenes in Agra, a city of fascination in its own right. It is not just the Taj Mahal.

the two-rupee tickets sold for admission to the Taj Mahal and other monuments.

At the time of writing, Agra was due for a revision of a thirty-year master plan designed to take it to the year 2000. So much has changed since it was drafted before 1971 that an entirely new job may be necessary, and then putting it into effect will be difficult. The tourists living in the hotel belt may not encounter Agra's congestion, but they will if they venture into parts of the old town still paved with slabs of

red stone, as in Akbar's time. The traffic jam in narrow lanes is almost permanent.

As an example of the city's problems, public transport has failed entirely to keep up with population. A town planner told me Agra had only fortytwo buses — and as a result, to fill the gap, had sixteen thousand rickshaws. Those which cluster around the tourist hotels are only a tiny fraction of the total. They provide better service than buses do, but hiring them costs more and they add to the traffic congestion. How do you remedy this? Buses are expensive and thousands of displaced rickshawmen would make trouble which no administrator would invite upon himself.

On the other hand — in India there is always another hand — life

People at the Taj Mahal can be as engaging as the monument. They come from all over India, and all over the world.

in crowded parts of the city need not be all that bad. Away from the hurly-burly of the streets, which many people enjoy anyway, you may find a sense of community absent in smarter and newer cities. Consider Tajganj, once known as Mumtazabad.

It is a densely populated area, with at least fifty thousand people, directly south of the Taj Mahal, and it dates back at least to the construction of the Taj. Some say it was built to house workers on the job, and it is certain that many families living there today believe they are descended from those workers.

At first sight Tajganj is interesting but perhaps not the sort of place you would choose to live in. Marching through its lanes you will find herds of big, black buffaloes, donkeys carrying sand and gravel, horse carts, goats, pigs in the drains, perhaps a camel or two. Some of the lanes are very narrow and many of the buildings show their considerable age.

But Tajganj is not a slum. The lanes are clean, the people alert and friendly, those ancient buildings not so bad after all. 'Everyone cleans the street in front of his house,' I was told. Many families have improved the interiors of their houses. Services are available in surprising degree — schools, hospitals, clinics. There are workshops and small factories making leather goods, inlaid marble work, jewellery, clothing, furniture. There is a complete economy in there.

This perfect and most lovely building infinitely surpassed all I had expected, principally on account of its size, and its colour. It is quite impossible to imagine a more beautiful or wonderful sight. . . . Descriptions of this wonderfully lovely place are simply silly, as no words can describe it at all. . . . Henceforth, let the inhabitants of the world be divided into two classes — them as has seen the Taj Mahal; and them as hasn't. — Edward Lear, most noted as a writer of nonsense poems, Indian Journal, 1874.

I was touched to find a device once used to raise a kerosene lamp to the top of its pole (no longer in use because electric street lights have been installed) now employed as a bird feeder. Several times a day the tray which has replaced the lamp is lowered, restocked with food and raised again. The area includes some acceptable guesthouses for tourists who want to live nearer to the Taj Mahal.

Still more interesting is the sense of community. By contrast with new housing areas where people are separated by fences, walls, status and suspicion, the people of the different communities within Tajganj have known and worked together all their lives and often are related as well. It is a trade off. Offer these people new and modern

houses and they would probably accept them; but moving would be at considerable cost to their way of life and sense of belonging. And it could also cost them their present privileged access to the Taj Mahal.

Whether in old houses or new, the people of Agra are the people of the Taj Mahal, familiar with it and proud of it. Often in conversation it is as if Shah Jahan and Mumtaz Mahal died only yesterday. The Taj has such immediacy in their lives that they take for granted all that it stands for.

After hearing its praises ever since I had been in India, its beauty rather exceeded than fell short of my expectations. — Reginald Heber, Bishop of Calcutta, about 1825.

It is in the nature of things that they do not visit the Taj often, but when they do they have a feeling for it all their own. The evening is a favourite time for Tajganj people to stroll in family groups up through the great south gate, across the forecourt and through the main entrance. The sun sinks into the haze above the horizon, frustrating photographers. Squirrels chitter and birds flash about in their pre-roosting rituals. The dome of the monument changes colour from minute to minute. Children rush about the lawns playing tag. Lovers — this being India — avoid holding hands. Shadows lengthen.

It is pleasant at such a time to sit on the central marble plinth, watching the people of the world drift towards the main gateway with many a backward glance. It is pleasant to think that the family sitting or strolling nearby perhaps has a direct link back through time to the people who built this monument, this 'spectacle of the highest celebrity'. You think of the story of the Taj, of Shah Jahan and Mumtaz Mahal, of how they came to lie together in death, of how their story continues to captivate.

The vast surrounding plains grow darker, the huge dome reddens along its western edges, and the parents call their running and laughing children to order. There is a magic in the air and you cease to think of anything in particular. Time stands still and three hundred years are compressed into an instant. It is a perfect place to end the day, and perhaps also a perfect place to end this book.

Index